The Kids' Guide to Birds of Washington

Fun Facts, Activities, and 88 Cool Birds

by Stan Tekiela

Adventure Publications
an imprint of AdventureKEEN

DEDICATION

To all the children who enjoy the world of birds as much as I do.

ACKNOWLEDGMENTS

Special thanks to the National Wildlife Refuge System along with state and local agencies, both public and private, for stewarding the lands that are critical to the many bird species we so love.

Edited by Jenna Barron, Dan Downing, Sandy Livoti, and Brett Ortler
Cover and book design by Jonathan Norberg
Illustrations by Elleyna Ruud
Range maps produced by Anthony Hertzel

Cover photos by Stan Tekiela. Front: Mountain Bluebird, Canada Jay, Wood Duck, Mountain Chickadee, Great Horned Owl, American Goldfinch, Wild Turkey. **Back:** Western Tanager

All photos by Stan Tekiela except pg. 60 (main) by **Paul Bannick**; pp. 92 (female), 188 (male), 190 (male), 212 (female) by **Rick & Nora Bowers**; pp. 82 (winter), 202 (juvenile & winter) by **Brian E. Small**; and pp. 34 (juvenile), 130 (juvenile), 164 (in-flight juvenile) by **Brian K. Wheeler**.

Images used under license from Shutterstock.com:
Adrian Eugen: 199; **Anatoliy Lukich:** 58 (inset), 60 (inset); **Birdiegal:** 186 (inset); **BlueBarronPhoto:** 118 (top inset); **Carl Olsen:** 41; **Carrie Olson:** 167; **Dr.Pixel:** 228; **drsuth48:** 217; **Erni:** 82 (main); **Glass and Nature:** 198 (top inset); **Harold Stiver:** 191; **J. Omar Hansen:** 188 (top inset), 220; **JamesChen:** 119; **Jeff W. Jarrett:** 135, 216 (inset); **Jeremy Borkat:** 118 (main), 166 (female); **John Rakestraw:** 202 (top inset); **Keneva Photography:** 189; **Lindsay Helms:** 221; **M. Leonard Photography:** 214 (female); **Matt Morrissette:** 190 (top inset); **Michael Woodruff:** 61; **Nick Pecker:** 82 (inset), 83; **Nina B:** 212 (top inset); **Paul Bryan:** 177; **punkbirdr:** 92 (top inset); **Richard G Smith:** 184 (main), 198 (male); **Risto Puranen:** 185; **Sari Oneal:** 72 (inset); **Steve Jamsa:** 206 (main); **Sundry Photography:** 54 (female); **Susan Hodgson:** 184 (top inset); **Thomas Morris:** 174 (female); **vagabond54:** 93, 176 (inset); **Wirestock Creators:** 166 (top inset); **WLB79:** 213; and **yhelfman:** 58 (main), 59.

To the best of the publisher's knowledge, all photos were of live birds. Some were photographed in a controlled condition.

10 9 8 7 6 5 4 3 2 1

The Kids' Guide to Birds of Washington: Fun Facts, Activities, and 88 Cool Birds

Published by Adventure Publications
An imprint of AdventureKEEN
310 Garfield Street South
Cambridge, Minnesota 55008
(800) 678-7006
www.adventurepublications.net

Printed in China
Cataloging-in-Publication data is available from the Library of Congress
ISBN 978-1-64755-460-6 (pbk.); ISBN 978-1-64755-461-3 (ebook)

Quick-Flip Color Guide

TABLE OF CONTENTS

Introduction

The Birds

Bird Food Fun for the Family

More Activities for the Bird-Minded

COOL BIRDS IN WASHINGTON

The *Kids' Guide to Birds of Washington* is a fun, easy-to-use guide for anyone interested in seeing and identifying birds. As a child, I spent hours of enjoyment watching birds come to a wooden feeder that my father built in our backyard. We were the only family in the neighborhood who fed birds, and we became known as the nature family.

Now, more people feed birds in their backyards than those who go hunting or fishing combined. Not only has it become very popular to feed and watch birds, but young and old alike are also identifying them and learning more about them.

Washington is a fantastic state to see all sorts of birds. In fact, more than 500 species are found here on a regular basis! That makes this one of the top places to watch an incredible variety of birds. In this field guide for Washington, I'm featuring 88 of the most common of these great species.

We have marvelous **habitats** in Washington that are perfect for birds. We have a great mix of habitats for a wide variety of birds. Each of our habitats supports different kinds of birds. Much of the state is covered with **coniferous** forests and we also have a temperate rainforest which is only found here. This is a great place to see Pine Siskins, Steller's Jays, and Mountain Chickadees. A good portion of the state has open lands or grassland which contains species such as Red-tailed Hawks and Meadowlarks.

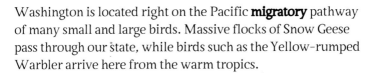

In addition to the forests and open space, Washington has some wonderful wetlands, rivers, ponds, lakes, and streams. We have many kinds of birds such as the Wood Duck and American Dipper that live here.

Washington is located right on the Pacific **migratory** pathway of many small and large birds. Massive flocks of Snow Geese pass through our state, while birds such as the Yellow-rumped Warbler arrive here from the warm tropics.

The weather here also plays a role in the kinds of birds we see. Bullock's Orioles nest here during summer. Migrating shore-birds, such as Killdeer, come to Washington to nest. On top of that, backyard birds, most notably Black-headed Grosbeaks and American Goldfinches, enjoy our seasons.

As you can see, Washington is a terrific place to watch all kinds of cool birds. It is my sincere hope that you and your family will like watching and feeding birds as much as I did with my family when I was a kid. Let this handy book guide you into a lifetime of appreciating birds and nature.

BODY BASICS OF A BIRD

It's good to know the names of a bird's body parts. The right terminology will help you describe and identify a bird when you talk about it with your friends and family.

The basic parts of a bird are labeled in the illustration below. This drawing is a combination (composite) of several birds and should not be regarded as one particular species.

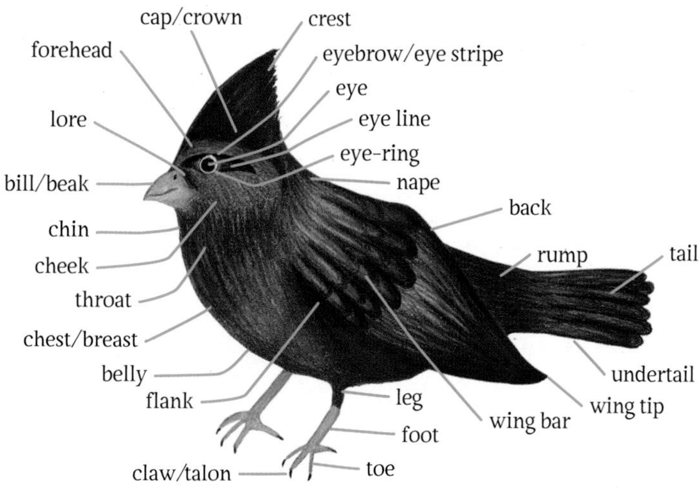

AMAZING NESTS

I am fascinated with bird nests! They are amazing structures that do more than just provide a place for egg laying. Nests create a small climate-controlled environment that's beneficial for both keeping the eggs warm and raising the young after they hatch.

From the high treetops to the ground, there are many kinds of nests. Some are simple, while others are complex. In any case, they function in nearly the same way. Nests help to contain the eggs so they don't roll away. They also help to keep baby birds warm on cold nights, cool on hot days, and dry during rains.

The following illustrations show the major types of nests that birds build in Washington.

GROUND **PLATFORM** **CUP** **PENDULOUS** **CAVITY**

A **ground nest** can be a mound of plant materials on the ground or in the water. Some are just a shallow spot scraped in the earth.

A **platform nest** is a cluster of sticks with a depression in the center. It is secured to the platform of a tree fork or to several tree branches.

A **cup nest** has a cupped interior, like a bowl.

A **pendulous nest** is a woven nest that hangs and swings freely, like a pendulum, from a branch.

A **cavity nest** is simply a cavity, or hole, usually in a tree.

The first step in nest building is to choose an appropriate site. Each bird species has a unique requirement for this. Some birds, such as American Robins, just need a tree branch. Others, like Western Bluebirds, look for a cavity and build the nest inside. Still others, such as Killdeer, search for camouflaged ground to scrape out a nest. Sometimes birds such as Turkey Vultures don't bother building a nest at all if they spot a hard-to-reach cliff or rocky ledge, where it will be safe to lay their eggs.

Nest materials usually consist of common natural items found in the area, like sticks or dried grass. Birds use other materials, such as mud or spiderwebs, to glue the materials together.

One of the amazing things about nest construction is that the parents don't need building plans or tool belts. They already know by instinct how to build nests, and they use their beaks and feet as their main tools.

To bring in nesting materials, birds must make many trips back and forth to the nest site. Most use their beaks to hold as much material as possible during each trip. Some of the bigger birds, like Bald Eagles, use larger materials, such as thick sticks and thin branches. They grasp and carry these items with their feet.

Nest building can take two to four days or longer, depending on the species and nest type. The simpler the nest, the faster the construction. Mourning Dove parents, for example, take just a few days to collect one to two dozen sticks for their platform nest. Woodpecker pairs, however, work upwards of a week to **excavate**, or dig out, a suitable nesting cavity. Large and more complicated platform nests, such as a Bald Eagle nest, may take weeks or even a month to complete, but these can be used for years and are worth the extra effort.

WHO BUILT THAT NEST?

In the majority of bird species, the chief builder is the female. In other species, both the female and the male typically share in the construction equally.

In general, when male and female birds look vastly different, the female does most of the work. When the male and female look alike or appear very similar, they tend to share the tasks of nest building and feeding the young. Alternatively, some species of woodpeckers have a different building plan. When they chisel out a nesting chamber, often the male does more of the work after the female has chosen the site.

ATTRACTING BIRDS WITH FEEDERS

To get more birds to visit your yard, an easy way to invite them is to put out bird feeders. Bird feeders are often as unique as the birds themselves, so the types of feeders you use really depends on the kinds of birds you're trying to attract.

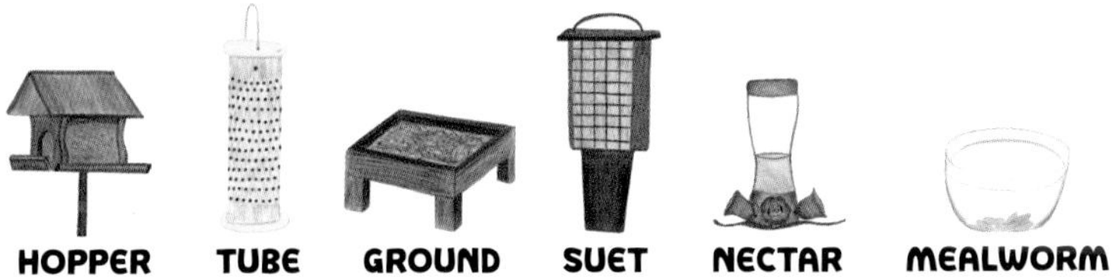

Hopper feeders are often wooden or plastic. Designed to hold a large amount of seeds, they often have a slender opening along the bottom, which dispenses the seeds. Birds land along the sides and help themselves to the food. Hopper feeders work well as main feeders in conjunction with other types of feeders. They are perfect for offering several kinds of seed mixes for finches, nuthatches, doves, and more.

Tube feeders with large seed ports and multiple perches are very popular. Often mostly plastic, they tend to be rugged enough to last several years and can be easily cleaned. These feeders are great for black oil sunflower seeds and seed mixes, which are favorites of nuthatches and all the other bird species that also visit hopper feeders.

Some tube feeders have small holes, allowing incredibly tiny thistle seeds to be dispensed just a few at a time. Use this kind of feeder to offer Nyjer seed, which will attract various finches.

Other styles of tube feeders have a wire mesh covering with openings large enough for birds to extract one of their favorite foods—peanuts out of the shell. Most birds enjoy peanuts, so these feeders will be some of the most popular in your yard. Another variety of tube feeder has openings large enough for peanuts in the shell. These are also very popular with the birds.

Ground feeders allow a wide variety of birds to access the food. The simplest and easiest feeders to use, they consist of a flat platform with a lip around the edges to keep seeds and corn from spilling out. Some have a roof to keep rain and snow off the food. With or without a roof, drainage holes in the bottom are important. Ground feeders will bring in towhees and many other birds to your backyard, including doves, and even mallards if you're near water.

Suet feeders are simply wire cages that hold cakes of **suet**. The wire allows woodpeckers, nuthatches, and other birds to cling securely to the feeder while pecking out chunks of suet. The best suet feeders have a vertical extension at the bottom where a woodpecker can brace its tail and support itself while feeding. These are called tail-prop suet feeders.

Nectar feeders are glass or plastic containers that hold sugar water. These feeders usually have plastic parts that are bright red, a color that is extremely attractive to hummingbirds, but orioles and woodpeckers will also stop for a drink. They often have up to four ports for access to the liquid and yellow bee guards to prevent bees from getting inside.

Mealworm feeders can be very basic—a simple glass or plastic cup or container will do. Pick one with sides tall enough and make sure the material is slippery enough to stop the lively mealworms from crawling out. Bluebirds especially love this wiggly treat!

HOW TO USE THIS GUIDE

Birds move pretty fast, so you don't often get a lot of time to observe them. To help you quickly find the birds in the book, this guide is organized by color. Simply note the most prominent color of the bird you've seen. A Downy Woodpecker, for example, is black and white and has a red mark on its head. Since this bird is mostly black and white, you would find it in the black and white section.

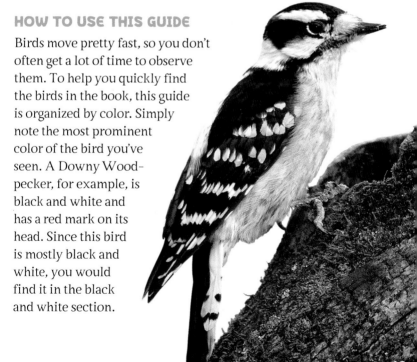

Within each color section, the birds are organized by size, from small to large. Use the Real Quick sidebar to find the size that your bird appears to be.

When the male and female of a species are different colors (like the Northern Shoveler pair below), they are shown in their own color sections. In these cases, the opposite sex is included in an inset photo with a page reference so you can easily turn to it.

If you already know the name of the bird you've seen, use the Checklist/Index to get the page number, and flip to it to learn more about the bird.

To further help you with identification, check the range maps to see where and when the bird you have sighted is normally in Washington. Range maps capture our current knowledge of where the birds are during a given year (presence) but do not

indicate how many birds are in the area (density). In addition, since birds fly around freely, it's possible to see them outside of their ranges. So please use the maps to get a general idea of where the birds are most likely to be seen.

For more about the information given for each bird in this guide, turn to the House Finch sample on pp. 16–17.

While you're learning about birds and identifying them, don't forget to check out the fun-filled things to do starting on pg. 220. Score a big hit with the birds in your yard by creating tasty treats or making your own bird food from the recipes. Put out some nesting materials to help birds build their nests. Consider signing up for a cool citizen science project suitable for the entire family. These are just a few of the activities that are such great fun, you'll want to do them all!

House Finch

Common name

Look for the reddish face and the brown cap

Field markings that help identify the bird

MALE

FEMALE
pg. 69

Color tab

Mostly Red

What to look for:
outstanding features; may include other **plumages** and descriptions

Where you'll find them:
where you're most likely to see the bird

Calls and songs:
songs, **calls** and other sounds the bird makes

On the move:
anything about flight, **flocks**, travel, and other movements

What they eat:
foods the bird eats and the kinds of feeders it visits

Nest:
type of nest; may include nest site, materials, and more

Eggs, chicks, and childcare:
number of eggs, color and marks; **incubation** and feeding duties; may include how many **broods**

Spends the winter:
where the bird goes when it's cold or when food is scarce

The bold word means it is defined in the glossary

REAL QUICK

Length from head to tail

Size
5"

Type of nest the bird calls home

Nest
CUP

Type of feeder the bird generally visits

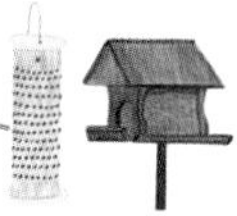

Feeder
TUBE OR HOPPER

Range map

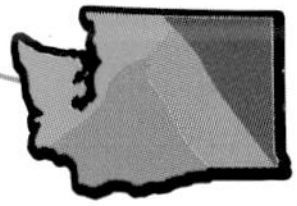

year-round
summer
migration
winter

After you've seen it, checkmark it

SAW IT!

STAN'S COOL STUFF

Fun and interesting facts about the bird. Information not typically found in other field guides.

Brown-headed Cowbird

Look for the brown head

MALE

FEMALE
pg. 89

What to look for:
glossy black bird with a chocolate-brown head and a sharp, pointed gray bill

Where you'll find them:
forest edges, open fields, farmlands, and backyards

Calls and songs:
sings a low, gurgling song that sounds like water moving; cowbird young are raised by other bird parents, but they still end up singing and calling like their own parents, whom they've never heard

On the move:
Mom flies quietly to another bird's nest, swiftly lays an egg, then flies quickly away

What they eat:
insects and seeds; visits seed feeders

Nest:
doesn't nest; lays eggs in the nests of other birds

Eggs, chicks, and childcare:
white eggs with brown marks; the **host** bird **incubates** any number of cowbird eggs in her nest and feeds the cowbird young along with her own

Spends the winter:
in southwestern states; some don't **migrate**

REAL QUICK

Size
7½"

Nest
NONE

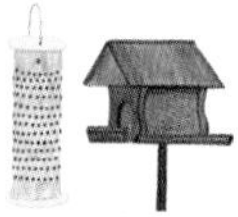

Feeder
TUBE OR HOPPER

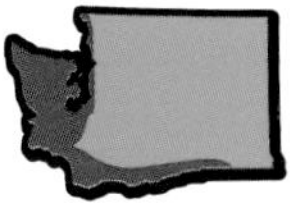

year-round
summer

SAW IT!

STAN'S COOL STUFF

Cowbirds are **brood parasites**, meaning they don't nest or raise their own families. Instead, they lay their eggs in other birds' nests, leaving the host birds to raise their young. Cowbirds have laid their eggs in the nests of more than 200 other bird species.

European Starling

Look for the glittering, iridescent feathers

What to look for:

shiny and **iridescent** purplish black in spring and summer, speckled in fall and winter; yellow bill in spring, gray in fall; pointed wings and a short tail

Where you'll find them:

lines up with other starlings on power lines; found in all **habitats** but usually associated with farms, suburban yards, and cities

Calls and songs:

mimics the songs of up to 20 bird species; mimics other sounds, even imitating the human voice

On the move:

large family groups gather with blackbirds in fall

What they eat:

bugs, seeds, and fruit; visits seed and **suet** feeders

Nest:

cavity; filled with dried grass; often takes a cavity from other birds

Eggs, chicks, and childcare:

4–6 bluish eggs with brown marks; Mom and Dad sit on the eggs and feed the babies

Spends the winter:

in Washington

REAL QUICK

Size
7½"

Nest
CAVITY

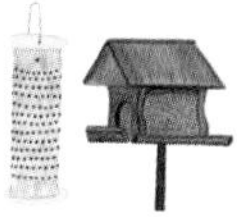

Feeder
TUBE OR HOPPER

year-round

SAW IT!

STAN'S COOL STUFF

The starling is a mimic that can sound like any other bird. It's not a native bird; 100 starlings from Europe were introduced to New York City in 1890–91. Today, European Starlings are one of the most common songbirds in the country.

Spotted Towhee

Look for the rusty red-brown sides

What to look for:
mostly black with rusty sides, a white belly, white spots on the wings, red eyes, and a long black tail with a white tip; female is very similar but with a brown head

Where to find them:
shrubby areas with short trees and thick bushes, backyards, and parks

Calls and songs:
calls "tow-hee" distinctly; also has a characteristic **call** that sounds like "drink-your-tea"

On the move:
short flights between shrubby areas and heavy **cover**; flashes white wing patches during flight

What they eat:
insects, seeds, and fruit; comes to ground feeders

Nest:
cup; Mom constructs the nest

Eggs, chicks, and childcare:
3–4 creamy-white eggs with brown marks; Mom **incubates** the eggs; Dad and Mom feed the young

Spends the winter:
in Washington; some **migrate** south

REAL QUICK

Size
8½"

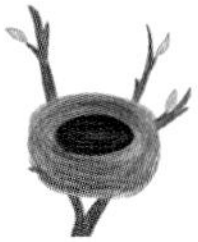

Nest
CUP

Feeder
GROUND

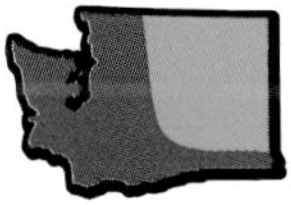

year-round
summer

SAW IT!

STAN'S COOL STUFF

The towhee is named for its distinctive "tow-hee" call. It hops backward with both feet, raking leaves to find insects and seeds. It is a large species of sparrow, nearly the size of a robin. It often has more than one clutch of eggs each breeding season.

Red-winged Blackbird

Look for the red-and-yellow shoulder patches

What to look for:
black bird with red-and-yellow shoulder patches on upper wings; shoulder patches can be partially or completely covered up

Where you'll find them:
around marshes, wetlands, lakes, and rivers

Calls and songs:
male sings and repeats **calls** from cattail tops and the surrounding **vegetation**

On the move:
flocks with as many as 10,000 birds gather in autumn, often with other blackbirds

What they eat:
seeds in spring and autumn, insects in summer; visits seed and **suet** feeders

Nest:
cup; in a thick stand of cattails over shallow water

Eggs, chicks, and childcare:
3–4 speckled bluish-green eggs; Mom does all the **incubating**, but both parents feed the babies

Spends the winter:
in Washington; moves around to find food

REAL QUICK

Size
8½"

Nest
CUP

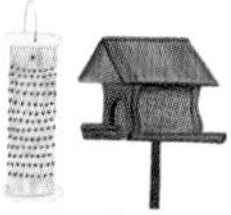

Feeder
TUBE OR HOPPER

year-round

SAW IT!

STAN'S COOL STUFF

During autumn and winter, thousands of these birds gather in farm fields, wetlands, and marshes. Come spring, males sing to defend territories and show off their wing patches (**epaulets**) to the females. Later, males can be aggressive when defending their nests.

Yellow-headed Blackbird

Look for the lemon-yellow head

What to look for:
black bird with a lemon-yellow head, neck, and chest, and a black mask

Where you'll find them:
around marshes, wetlands, and lakes

Calls and songs:
usually heard before it is seen; gives a low, raspy, metallic-sounding **call**

On the move:
migrates in **flocks** of up to 200 blackbirds; flocks of mainly males return in April before the females

What they eat:
insects and seeds; comes to ground feeders

Nest:
cup in a deep-water marsh, in a large **colony** with 20–100 other nests

Eggs, chicks, and childcare:
3–5 speckled greenish-white eggs; Mom **incubates** the eggs and feeds the chicks

Spends the winter:
in southwestern states and Mexico, often with Red-winged Blackbirds (pg. 25) and Brown-headed Cowbirds (pg. 19)

REAL QUICK

Size
9–11"

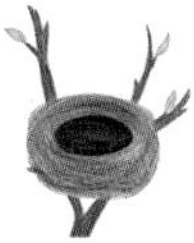

Nest
CUP

Feeder
GROUND

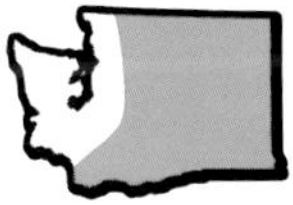

summer

SAW IT!

STAN'S COOL STUFF

The male performs a mating **display** in flight and when perched. He displays in flight with his head drooped, and his feet and tail pointing down. When perched, he throws his head back and calls. The young stay hidden for up to three weeks before starting to fly.

American Coot

Look for the white bill

What to look for:
gray-to-black with a duck-like white bill, red eyes

Where you'll find them:
in large **flocks** on open water

Calls and songs:
a unique series of creaks, groans, and clicks

On the move:
bobs head while swimming; takes off from water by scrambling across it with wings flapping; huge flocks of up to 1,000 birds gather for **migration**; migrates at night

What they eat:
insects and aquatic plants

Nest:
ground nest floating in water, anchored to plants

Eggs, chicks, and childcare:
9–12 speckled pinkish-tan eggs; Mom and Dad sit on the eggs and feed the **hatchlings**

Spends the winter:
in western coastal US, Mexico, and Central America; some stay in Washington

REAL QUICK

Size
13-16"

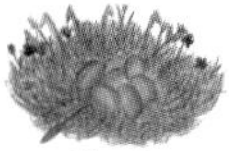

Nest
GROUND

Feeder
NONE

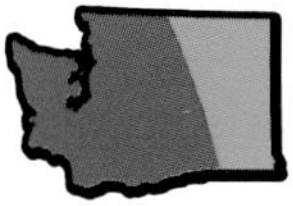

year-round
summer

SAW ☑ IT!

STAN'S COOL STUFF

The coot is not a duck. Instead of webbed feet, it has large lobed toes! It's smaller than most other **waterfowl**, and it is a great diver and swimmer. You won't see it flying, but you may spot one trying to escape from a Bald Eagle (pg. 49). It's also called a Mud Hen.

American Crow

Look for the glossy black feathers

What to look for:
glossy black all over and a black bill

Where you'll find them:
all **habitats**—wilderness, rural, suburban, cities

Calls and songs:
a harsh "caw" **call**; imitates other birds and people

On the move:
flaps constantly and glides downward; moves around to find food; gathers in huge communal **flocks** of more than 10,000 birds during winter

What they eat:
fruit, insects, mammals, fish, and dead carcasses (**carrion**); visits seed and **suet** feeders

Nest:
platform; adds bright or shiny items and often uses the same site every year if a Great Horned Owl (pg. 129) hasn't taken it

Eggs, chicks, and childcare:
4–6 speckled bluish-to-olive eggs; Mom sits on the eggs; Mom and Dad feed the youngsters

Spends the winter:
in Washington

REAL QUICK

Size
18"

Nest
PLATFORM

Feeder
HOPPER

year-round

SAW IT!

STAN'S COOL STUFF

The crow is one of the smartest of all birds. It's very social and often entertains itself by chasing other birds. It eats roadkill but avoids being hit by vehicles. Some can live as long as 20 years! Crows without mates, called helpers, help to raise the young.

Common Raven

Look for the large thick bill

What to look for:
black with a shaggy beard of feathers on throat and chin; long feathers on legs make it look like it's wearing pants

Where you'll find them:
remote or wilderness settings and also cities

Calls and songs:
a deep, raspy **call** that's lower-pitched than a crow's call; has more pops and unusual calls than a crow

On the move:
known for its aerial acrobatics and long swooping dives; able to soar on **thermals**

What they eat:
insects, fruit, small animals, and **carrion**, especially roadkill

Nest:
platform; Mom and Dad build at the same site for many years

Eggs, chicks, and childcare:
4–6 pale-green eggs with brown marks; Mom **incubates** while Dad brings food

Spends the winter:
in Washington

REAL QUICK

Size
22–27"

Nest
PLATFORM

Feeder
NONE

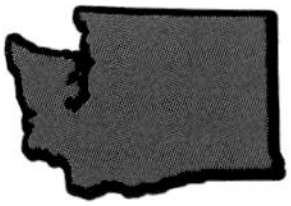

year-round

SAW IT!

STAN'S COOL STUFF

The Common Raven may be the smartest bird. When ravens find food, they share information with family members where to find it. Ravens build a large nest out of sticks; some nests can be several feet wide and are used for many years in a row.

Turkey Vulture

Look for the naked red head

What to look for:
naked red head and legs and an ivory bill; **juvenile** has a gray-to-blackish head and bill

Where you'll find them:
in trees, sunning itself with wings outstretched while drying after a rain

Calls and songs:
mostly **mute**, just grunts and groans

On the move:
holds wings in an upright V in flight, teetering from wing tip to wing tip as it soars and hovers

What they eat:
carrion; parents **regurgitate** food for their young

Nest:
no nest, or in a minimal nest on a cliff, in a cave, or even sometimes in a hollow tree trunk

Eggs, chicks, and childcare:
1–3 white eggs with brown marks; Mom and Dad **incubate** the eggs and feed the baby vultures

Spends the winter:
in southwestern states, Mexico, and Central and South America

REAL QUICK

Size
26–32"

Nest
NONE

Feeder
NONE

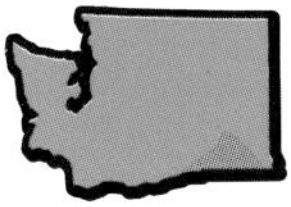

summer
migration

SAW IT!

STAN'S COOL STUFF

This is one of the few birds with a good sense of smell. It has a strong bill for tearing apart flesh. Unlike hawks and eagles, it has weak feet more suited for walking than grasping wiggly **prey**. The bare head reduces its risk of getting diseases from carcasses.

Double-crested Cormorant

Look for the large, hooked bill

What to look for:
large black waterbird with unusual blue eyes, a long snake-like neck, and a large gray bill with a yellow base and hooked tip

Where you'll find them:
usually roosts in large groups in trees near water

Calls and songs:
grunts, pops, and groans—none are pleasant sounds at all!

On the move:
swims underwater to catch fish, holding its wings at its sides; flies in a large V-shaped formation

What they eat:
small fish and aquatic insects

Nest:
platform; near or over open water, in a **colony**

Eggs, chicks, and childcare:
3–4 bluish-white eggs; parents take turns sitting on the eggs and feeding the young

Spends the winter:
in western coastal US; some don't **migrate**

REAL QUICK

Size
31-35"

Nest
PLATFORM

Feeder
NONE

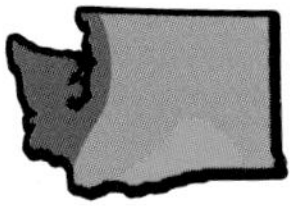

year-round
summer
migration

SAW IT!

STAN'S COOL STUFF

This bird's outer feathers are different from its inner ones; the outer feathers soak up water, but its body feathers don't. It opens its wings and uses the sun and wind to dry out. "Double-crested" refers to the two unusual crests on its head, but these aren't often seen.

Downy Woodpecker

Look for the small, short bill

What to look for:
spotted wings, white belly, red mark on the back of the head, and a small, short bill; female lacks a red mark on the head

Where you'll find them:
wherever trees are present

Calls and songs:
repeats a high-pitched "peek-peek" **call**; drums on trees or logs with its bill to announce its territory

On the move:
flies in an up-and-down pattern; makes short flights from tree to tree

What they eat:
insects and seeds; visits **suet** and seed feeders

Nest:
cavity in a dead tree; digs out a perfectly round entrance hole; the bottom of the cavity is wider than the top, and it's lined with fallen woodchips

Eggs, chicks, and childcare:
3–5 white eggs; Mom **incubates** the eggs; both parents take care of the kiddies

Spends the winter:
in Washington

REAL QUICK

Size
6"

Nest
CAVITY

Feeder
SUET

year-round

SAW ☑ IT!

STAN'S COOL STUFF

The Downy is abundant and widespread where trees are present. Like other woodpeckers, it pulls insects from tiny places with its long, barbed tongue. It has stiff tail feathers, which help to support it as it clings to trees. During winter, it will roost in a cavity.

Red-breasted Sapsucker

Look for the white mark over the bill

What to look for:
black and white body, wings, and tail; white-to-pale-yellow belly; red head, chest, and nape; white mark over bill

Where you'll find them:
deciduous forest at higher elevations

Calls and songs:
a high-pitched "phew, phew"; slow, irregular drumming pattern

On the move:
direct flight directly to trunk of tree

What they eat:
insects, tree **sap**, and berries

Nest:
cavity; Mom and Dad build it

Eggs, chicks, and childcare:
3–7 white eggs; Mom and Dad **incubate** the eggs and feed the babies

Spends the winter:
in Washington; moves around to find food

REAL QUICK

Size
8½"

Nest
CAVITY

Feeder
NONE

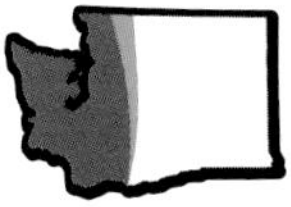

year-round
summer

SAW IT!

STAN'S COOL STUFF

This bird is a primary cavity nester, which means that other species of birds will use their nest cavity after they are done with it. They drill a row of holes from which sap seeps. This attracts insects, and the sapsucker feeds on the sap and the insects.

Pileated Woodpecker

Look for the bright red crest

What to look for:
bright red crest that looks like a hat; bright red forehead and mustache, and a black back; female has a black forehead and lacks a red mustache

Where you'll find them:
prefers areas with lots of woodland

Calls and songs:
drums on hollow branches, chimneys, and such to announce territory; loud, rapid "cuk-cuk-cuk" **calls** carry over a long distance

On the move:
white leading edge of wings flashes brightly during flight

What they eat:
insects (especially its favorite, carpenter ants); visits **suet** feeders and feeders with peanuts

Nest:
cavity in a dead or live tree trunk

Eggs, chicks, and childcare:
3–5 white eggs; Mom and Dad sit on the eggs and **regurgitate** bugs to feed the youngsters

Spends the winter:
moves around Washington to find food

REAL QUICK

Size
19"

Nest
CAVITY

Feeder
SUET

year-round

SAW IT!

STAN'S COOL STUFF

This is our largest woodpecker. It's shy, despite its size. It digs oval holes up to a few feet long in tree trunks, looking for bugs to eat. You'll see large wood chips at the base of those trees. The young come out of the nest looking and sounding just like the adults.

Black-billed Magpie

What to look for:

a large black-and-white bird with a very long tail, white belly, black legs, large black bill, and white wing patches that flash in flight; wings and tail are **iridescent** green in direct sunlight

Where you'll find them:

open and rural country

Calls and songs:

very vocal bird; its two primary **calls** are a harsh chatter and a raspy chatter

On the move:

quick flaps followed by a long glide; a long streaming tail

What they eat:

insects, **carrion**, fruit, and seeds

Nest:

modified pendulous; Mom and Dad build it

Eggs, chicks, and childcare:

5–8 green eggs with brown marks; Mom **incubates** the eggs, Mom and Dad and feed the babies

Spends the winter:

doesn't **migrate;** spends all year in Washington

REAL QUICK

Size
20"

Nest
PENDULOUS

Feeder
GROUND

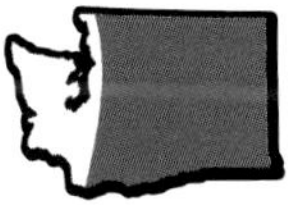

year-round

SAW IT!

STAN'S COOL STUFF

The Magpie is a very intelligent bird that is related to crows and jays. It makes a large dome nest deep within thick shrubs. They often travel in small family **flocks** with Mom and Dad, brothers, and sisters. They are a good mimic of other animals, including dogs and cats.

Osprey

Look for the dark line through the eyes

What to look for:
white chest, belly, and head, with a dark eye line

Where you'll find them:
always near water, from rivers to wetlands

Calls and songs:
a high-pitched, whistle-like **call**, often given in flight as a warning

On the move:
can hover for a few seconds before diving to catch a fish; carries fish in a head-first position in flight for better aerodynamics

What they eat:
fish

Nest:
platform made with twigs; on a raised wooden platform, man-made tower, or in a tall dead tree

Eggs, chicks, and childcare:
2–4 white eggs with brown marks; parents sit on the eggs and feed the **hatchlings**

Spends the winter:
in southern states, Mexico, Central America, and South America

REAL QUICK

Size
21–24"

Nest
PLATFORM

Feeder
NONE

summer

SAW IT!

STAN'S COOL STUFF

The Osprey is the only species in its family. It is the only **raptor** that plunges feet-first into the water to catch fish. Bald Eagles (pg. 49) will harass it for its catch. At one time, it was almost extinct. It was reintroduced to many regions, and populations are now stable.

Bald Eagle

Look for the white head

JUVENILE

What to look for:
white head and tail, curved yellow bill, and yellow feet; **juvenile** has white speckles and a gray bill

Where you'll find them:
often near water; likes open areas with daily food

Calls and songs:
weak, high-pitched screams, one after another

On the move:
a spectacular aerial mating **display** in which one eagle flips upside down and locks talons with another; both fall, tumbling down, then break apart and fly off

What they eat:
fish, **carrion**, and birds (prefers American Coots)

Nest:
massive platform of sticks, usually in a tree; nests used for many years can weigh up to 1,000 pounds

Eggs, chicks, and childcare:
2–3 off-white eggs; Mom and Dad share all duties

Spends the winter:
in Washington; moves around in winter to find food

REAL QUICK

Size
31–37"

Nest
PLATFORM

Feeder
NONE

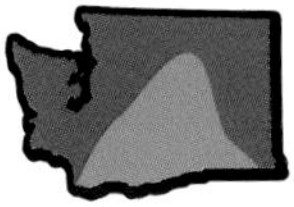

year-round
winter

SAW ⟨✓⟩ IT!

STAN'S COOL STUFF

Bald Eagles nearly became extinct, but they're doing well now. Their wingspan is huge, stretching out up to 7½ feet! They return to the same nest and add more sticks each year, enlarging it over time. The heads and tails of **juveniles** turn white at 4–5 years.

Tree Swallow

Look for the white chin and chest

What to look for:
blue-green bird with a white chin, chest, and belly, and long, pointed wings

Where you'll find them:
ponds, lakes, rivers, and farm fields

Calls and songs:
gives a series of gurgles and chirps; chatters when upset or threatened

On the move:
flies back and forth across fields, feeding on bugs; uses rapid wingbeats, and then glides; family units gather in large **flocks** for **migration**

What they eat:
insects—big and small

Nest:
cavity; adds grass and lines it with feathers; uses an old woodpecker hole or a wooden nest box

Eggs, chicks, and childcare:
4–6 white eggs; Mom sits on the eggs; Mom and Dad bring bugs to feed the babies

Spends the winter:
in Mexico and Central America

REAL QUICK

Size
5–6"

Nest
CAVITY

Feeder
NONE

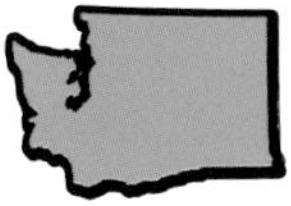

summer

SAW IT!

STAN'S COOL STUFF

A good bird to have around because it eats many bugs. You can attract it with a nest box; but it will compete with Mountain Bluebirds (pg. 53) for the cavity. It finds dropped feathers to line its nest and plays with them on its way back to the nest.

Mountain Bluebird

Look for the blue head, back, wings and tail

MALE

FEMALE

What to look for:

male is a sky-blue bird with a darker-blue head, back, wings, and tail and a white lower belly; thin black bill; female is tan with blue on the wings and tail

Where you'll find them:

open mountainous country, prairies, and fields

Calls and songs:

a simple **warbling** "churr," over and over

On the move:

perches while hunting; makes short direct flights

What they eat:

insects

Nest:

cavity; old woodpecker cavity, wooden nest box; Mom lines the cavity, making a cup for the eggs

Eggs, chicks, and childcare:

4–6 pale-blue eggs without markings; Mom sits on eggs; Mom and Dad feed the young

Spends the winter:

in Arizona, California, and Mexico

REAL QUICK

Size
7"

Nest
CAVITY

Feeder
MEALWORM

summer

SAW IT!

STAN'S COOL STUFF

Not that long ago, bluebirds were in trouble because people cut down the dead trees bluebirds often use for their nests. Thankfully, bluebirds adapt well to nest boxes, and over the last 50 years, people have placed many of them, helping their populations recover.

Western Bluebird

Look for the rusty-red chest and flanks

MALE

FEMALE

What to look for:
male has a deep-blue head, neck, throat, back, wings, and tail, and a rusty-red chest and flanks; female is duller overall and has a gray head

Where you'll find them:
open **habitats** (prefers farm fields, pastures, and roadsides), forest edges, parks, and yards

Calls and songs:
a soft "kew" given from a perch

On the move:
fast flight in open country to low perches

What they eat:
insects, fruit; visits mealworm and **suet** feeders

Nest:
cavity; adds a soft lining in an old woodpecker hole or a bluebird nest box; Mom builds it

Eggs, chicks, and childcare:
4–6 pale-blue eggs; Mom **incubates** the eggs, and Dad and Mom feed the kids

Spends the winter:
in Arizona, California, and Mexico

REAL QUICK

Size
7"

Nest
CAVITY

Feeder
MEALWORM

summer

SAW ✓ **IT!**

STAN'S COOL STUFF

Western Bluebirds are a familiar bird of open land or woodland edges. They eat mainly insects in the summer and fruit in the winter. Bluebirds nest in existing tree cavities, such as natural openings or old woodpecker holes, but they also come to nest boxes.

Barn Swallow

Look for the deeply forked tail

What to look for:
sleek blue-black back, rusty chin, cinnamon belly, and a long, deeply forked tail

Where you'll find them:
wetlands, farms, suburban yards, and parks

Calls and songs:
gives a twittering **warble** that's followed by a rapid mechanical sound

On the move:
flaps continuously, often low over land or water; unlike other swallows, it rarely glides

What they eat:
bugs—especially beetles, wasps (caught carefully), and flies

Nest:
cup made of mud; brings in up to 1,000 beak-loads of mud to build nest, often on a building; usually it's in a **colony** of 4–6 birds; sometimes nests alone

Eggs, chicks, and childcare:
4–5 white eggs with brown marks; Mom sits on the eggs, and Mom and Dad feed the chicks

Spends the winter:
in Central and South America

REAL QUICK

Size
7"

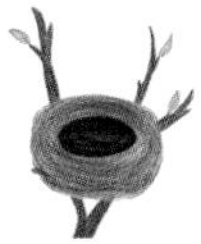

Nest
CUP

Feeder
NONE

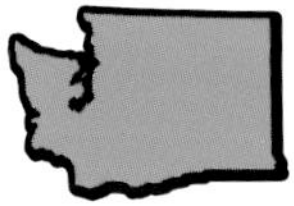

summer

SAW IT!

STAN'S COOL STUFF

The Barn Swallow is the only swallow in Washington with a deeply forked tail. It drinks while flying low over water, and it sips the waterdrops on wet leaves. It bathes when it flies through rain or sprinklers. Usually it nests on a barn, house, or under a bridge.

California Scrub-Jay

Look for the brownish patch on the back

What to look for:
deep-blue head, wings, tail, and breast band; a brownish patch on the back; a dull white chin, breast, and belly; and a very long tail

Where you'll find them:
oak woodlands, suburban yards, and parks

Calls and songs:
very vocal and loud; has many different harsh squeaks and other **calls**

On the move:
quick wingbeats straight to a perch

What they eat:
insects, seeds, and fruit; comes to seed feeders

Nest:
cup; Mom and Dad build it

Eggs, chicks, and childcare:
3–6 pale-green eggs with red-brown marks; Mom sits on the eggs; Mom and Dad feed the young

Spends the winter:
in Washington

REAL QUICK

Size
11"

Nest
CUP

Feeder
HOPPER

year-round

SAW ✓ IT!

STAN'S COOL STUFF

California Scrub-Jay and Woodhouse's Scrub-Jay were once considered the same species, but they were split into two separate species in 2016. California Scrub-Jays are often seen in small **flocks**. They feed on insects in spring and summer and on nuts in fall and winter.

Steller's Jay

Look for the black head and crest

What to look for:
dark-blue wings, tail, and belly; a black head, **nape**, and breast; and a pointed black crest on the head that can be lifted at will

Where you'll find them:
mainly in **coniferous** forests

Calls and songs:
a loud repeated "wheek, wheek, wheek" and a wide variety of gurgling sounds

On the move:
short, quick flight from perch to perch

What they eat:
insects, berries, and seeds; will visit seed feeders

Nest:
cup; Mom and Dad build it

Eggs, chicks, and childcare:
3–5 pale-green eggs with brown marks; Mom sits on the eggs; Mom and Dad feed the babies

Spends the winter:
in Washington; moves around to find food and shelter

REAL QUICK

Size
11"

Nest
CUP

Feeder
HOPPER

year-round

SAW IT!

STAN'S COOL STUFF

Steller's Jays in Washington tend to have blue streaks on their head and crest, while ones to the east of the Rockies tend to have white streaks. They carry many seeds in their bill and bury them one by one for winter use. Sometimes they come to people looking for food.

Belted Kingfisher

Look for the large, ragged crest

MALE

FEMALE

What to look for:
broad blue band on a white chest, ragged crest; female has a rusty band below her blue band

Where you'll find them:
rarely away from water; usually at banks of rivers, lakes, and large streams

Calls and songs:
gives a loud **call** that sounds like a machine gun rattling; mates know each other's call

On the move:
flashes the small white patches on its dark wing tips during flight

What they eat:
small fish

Nest:
cavity in the bank of a river, lake, or cliff; digs a tunnel up to 4 feet long to the nest chamber

Eggs, chicks, and childcare:
6–7 white eggs; Mom and Dad sit on the eggs and feed fish to their youngsters

Spends the winter:
in Washington; moves around to find food in winter

REAL QUICK

Size
12–14"

Nest
CAVITY

Feeder
NONE

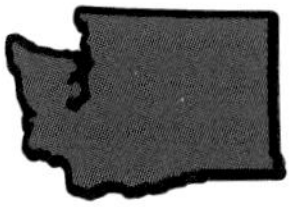

year-round

SAW IT!

STAN'S COOL STUFF

Belted Kingfishers perch near water and dive in headfirst to catch fish. Parents drop dead fish into the water to teach their young to dive. Kingfishers have short legs with two toes fused together. This helps a lot when they dig (**excavate**) a burrow for nesting.

Chipping Sparrow

Look for the rusty crown

What to look for:
gray-brown bird with a clear gray chest, white eyebrows, thin black eye line, and a rusty crown

Where you'll find them:
forest edges, suburban yards, parks, and openings in the forest

Calls and songs:
male gives a very long, dry, and fast "chip" **call**, repeating it over and over

On the move:
gathers and feeds in large family groups in preparation for migration; **flocks** of 20–30 birds **migrate** at night

What they eat:
insects and seeds; comes to ground feeders

Nest:
cup, usually lining it with animal hair; builds nest low in dense shrubs

Eggs, chicks, and childcare:
3–5 speckled blue-green eggs; Mom **incubates** the eggs; Mom and Dad share the childcare

Spends the winter:
in southwestern states, Mexico, and Central America

REAL QUICK

Size
5"

Nest
CUP

Feeder
GROUND

summer

SAW IT!

STAN'S COOL STUFF

This sparrow is a common garden or backyard bird, often dining on dropped seeds beneath feeders. Usually it isn't very afraid of people, so you may be able to come near it before it flies away. It is named for its quick "chip" call, and it's also known just as Chippy.

Pine Siskin

Look for the yellow on the wings

What to look for:
brown with a heavily streaked back, chest, and belly; yellow wing bars; and yellow at base of tail

Where you'll find them:
coniferous to **deciduous** forests, open fields

Calls and songs:
gives a series of high-pitched, wheezy **calls**; also gives a wheezing **twitter**

On the move:
moves around to visit feeders in **flocks** of up to 20 or more birds, often with other finch species; flashes yellow wing markings in flight

What they eat:
seeds, bugs; visits seed (especially thistle) feeders

Nest:
cup; builds nest in a conifer near the end of a branch, where needles are dense

Eggs, chicks, and childcare:
3–4 speckled greenish-blue eggs; Mom **incubates** the eggs; Mom and Dad bring food to the kiddies

Spends the winter:
in Washington; moves around in winter to find food

REAL QUICK

Size
5"

Nest
CUP

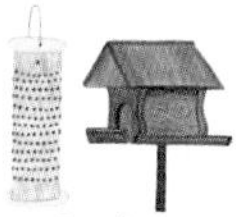

Feeder
TUBE OR HOPPER

year-round
winter

SAW IT!

STAN'S COOL STUFF

The Pine Siskin is a finch that breeds in small groups. Nests in the group are often only a few feet apart. The male feeds the female during incubation. **Juveniles** have a yellow tint on their chests and chins, but they lose this by late summer of their first year.

House Finch

Look for the heavily streaked chest

What to look for:
brown bird with heavy streaks on a white chest

Where you'll find them:
forests, city and suburban areas, around homes, parks, and farms

Calls and songs:
male sings a loud, cheerful **warbling** song

On the move:
moves around in small family units; never travels long distances

What they eat:
seeds, fruit, and leaf buds; comes to seed feeders and feeders with a glop of grape jelly

Nest:
cup; but occasionally in a cavity; likes to nest in a hanging flower basket or on a front door wreath

Eggs, chicks, and childcare:
4–5 pale-blue eggs, lightly marked; Mom sits on the eggs and Dad feeds her while she **incubates**; Mom and Dad feed the **brood**

Spends the winter:
in Washington

REAL QUICK

Size
5"

Nest
CUP

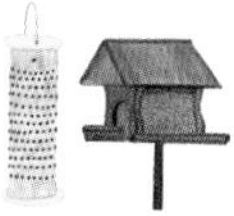

Feeder
TUBE OR HOPPER

year-round

SAW IT!

STAN'S COOL STUFF

The House Finch is very social and can be a common bird at feeders. It was introduced to New York from the western US in the 1940s. Now it's found all across the country. Unfortunately, it suffers from a fatal eye disease that causes the eyes to crust over.

House Wren

Look for the slightly curved bill

What to look for:
brown bird with light-brown marks on the wings and tail; a slightly curved brown bill

Where you'll find them:
brushy yards, woodlands, forest edges, and parks

Calls and songs:
sings a lot; during the mating season, it sings from dawn to dusk

On the move:
short flights from protective bushes; holds its tail up briefly after landing

What they eat:
insects, spiders, and snails

Nest:
cavity in a tree or birdhouse; easily attracted to a nest box; builds a twiggy nest in spring and lines it with pine needles and grass

Eggs, chicks, and childcare:
4–6 tan eggs with brown marks; Mom and Dad **incubate** the eggs and raise the chicks

Spends the winter:
in southwestern states and Mexico

REAL QUICK

Size
5"

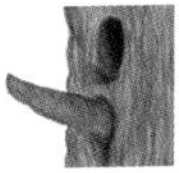

Nest
CAVITY

Feeder
NONE

summer

SAW ✓ IT!

STAN'S COOL STUFF

The male chooses several nest cavities and puts a few small twigs in each. The female selects one cavity, and then fills it with short twigs. Often she will have trouble fitting long twigs through the entrance hole, but she'll try again and again until she's successful.

Bewick's Wren

Look for the white chin and eyebrows

What to look for:
brown cap, back, wings, and tail; gray chest and belly; white chin and eyebrows; a pointed down-curved bill; and a long tail with white spots; often holds its tail up and wags it from side to side

Where you'll find them:
backyards, gardens, and shrubby areas

Calls and songs:
many different songs, with two or more high notes followed by a **trill**

On the move:
creeps around in **cover;** males sing from perches

What they eat:
insects and seeds

Nest:
cavity; Mom and Dad team up to build it

Eggs, chicks, and childcare:
4–8 white eggs with brown marks; Mom sits on the eggs; Mom and Dad feed for the youngsters

Spends the winter:
in parts of Washington

REAL QUICK

Size
5½"

Nest
CAVITY

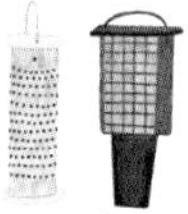

Feeder
TUBE OR SUET

year-round
winter

SAW IT!

STAN'S COOL STUFF

Bewick's Wrens are acrobatic birds often seen hanging upside down while hunting for insects. They will nest on rock ledges, and in brush piles, old woodpecker holes, and nest boxes. Multiple males may gather close to each other and sing to defend their territories.

Dark-eyed Junco

Look for the ivory-to-pink bill

pg. 147

What to look for:
plump bird with a tan-to-brown chest, head, and back; a white belly; and a tiny ivory-to-pink bill

Where you'll find them:
on the ground in small **flocks** with other juncos and sparrows

Calls and songs:
a beautiful, loud, musical **trill** lasting 2–3 seconds

On the move:
outermost tail feathers are white and appear as a white V during flight

What they eat:
seeds (scarfs down many weed seeds) and insects; visits ground and seed feeders

Nest:
cup on the ground in a wide variety of **habitats;** female chooses a well-hidden nest site

Eggs, chicks, and childcare:
3–5 white eggs with reddish-brown marks; Mom **incubates** the eggs; Dad and Mom feed the babies

Spends the winter:
in much of Washington; moves around to find food

REAL QUICK

Size
5½"

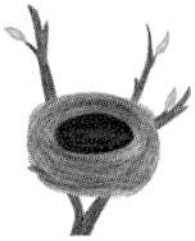

Nest
CUP

Feeder
GROUND

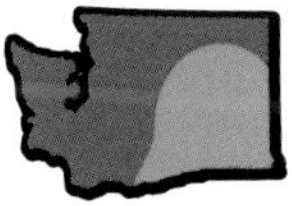

year-round
winter

SAW IT!

STAN'S COOL STUFF

The junco is a common year-round bird. Usually just the females are seen because they **migrate** farther south. This round, dark-eyed bird uses both feet at the same time to "**double-scratch**" the ground, exposing seeds and insects to eat.

House Sparrow

Look for the black throat patch

MALE

FEMALE

What to look for:
male has a brown back, gray belly and crown, and large black patch from throat to chest; female is light-brown with distinct light eyebrows and lacks a throat patch

Where you'll find them:
just about any **habitat**, from cities to farms

Calls and songs:
one of the first birds heard in cities during spring

On the move:
nearly always in small **flocks**

What they eat:
seeds, insects, and fruit; comes to seed feeders

Nest:
cavity; uses dried grass, scraps of plastic, paper, and whatever else is available to construct an oversized domed cup within the cavity

Eggs, chicks, and childcare:
4–6 white eggs with brown marks; Mom sits on the eggs; Mom and Dad feed the little ones

Spends the winter:
in Washington; doesn't **migrate**

REAL QUICK

Size
6"

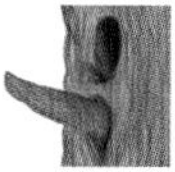

Nest
CAVITY

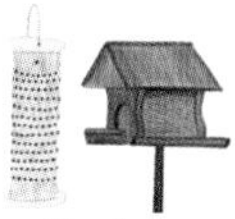

Feeder
TUBE OR HOPPER

year-round

SAW IT!

STAN'S COOL STUFF

The House Sparrow is very comfortable being around people. It was introduced to Central Park in New York City from Europe in 1850. It adjusted to nearly all habitats and now is seen across North America. Populations are decreasing in the US and worldwide.

Purple Finch

Look for the heavily streaked chest

MALE
pg. 197

What to look for:
brown bird with streaking on white chest and belly, strong white eyebrow

Where you'll find them:
suburban areas, around homes, parks, and forests

Calls and songs:
male sings a clear cheerful song

On the move:
in **flocks** in winter; pairs in nesting season

What they eat:
seeds, fruit, and insects; comes to seed feeders

Nest:
cup; often on far end of **conifer** branch or close to trunk in **deciduous** trees

Eggs, chicks, and childcare:
4–5 greenish-blue eggs with brown marks; Mom **incubates** the eggs; Mom and Dad feed the kids

Spends the winter:
in Washington; moves around to find food

REAL QUICK

Size
6"

Nest
CUP

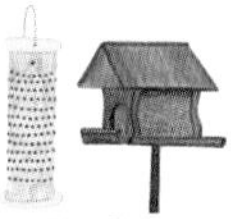

Feeder
TUBE OR HOPPER

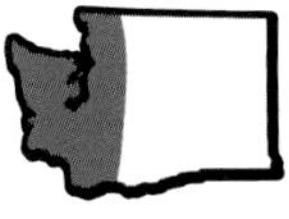

year-round

SAW IT!

STAN'S COOL STUFF

A highly migratory bird that moves around a lot in winter. Often comes to feeders in groups of males and females. Large bill helps crack open seeds to extract the nut.

White-throated Sparrow

Look for the light stripes on the head

MALE

FEMALE

What to look for:
striped head, white or tan throat patch, and small yellow **lores** between the eyes

Where you'll find them:
bogs, evergreen and leafy forests, under feeders

Calls and songs:
sings a wonderful song all year and can even be heard at night, sounding like "oh-Canada, Canada"

On the move:
often hangs around on the ground with other sparrows during winter

What they eat:
insects, seeds, and fruit; comes to ground feeders

Nest:
cup on the ground under a small tree

Eggs, chicks, and childcare:
4–6 greenish, bluish, or creamy-white eggs with reddish-brown marks; Mom **incubates** the eggs; Mom and Dad both take care of the babies

Spends the winter:
in Washington and southwestern states

REAL QUICK

Size
6–7"

Nest
CUP

Feeder
GROUND

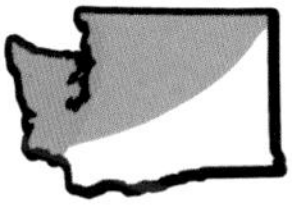

migration
winter

SAW IT!

STAN'S COOL STUFF

This bird has two color variations: white-striped and tan-striped. Both variations mate with each other. Both variations also sing, except for the tan-striped females. This is odd, and scientists aren't sure why those females don't sing. Maybe you can figure it out.

Golden-crowned Sparrow

Look for the yellow patch on the head

What to look for:
a typical-looking sparrow with a black-and-yellow stripe on head

Where you'll find them:
shrubs, forests

Calls and songs:
several clear notes, dropping downward in pitch

On the move:
often seen on ground with other sparrows, skulking around in shrubs

What they eat:
seeds, berries, and insects

Nest:
cup nest on the ground or in a shrub

Eggs, chicks, and childcare:
3–5 bluish-white eggs with brown marks; Mom **incubates** the eggs; Mom and Dad feed the kids

Spends the winter:
in Washington

REAL QUICK

Size
7"

Nest
CUP

Feeder
GROUND

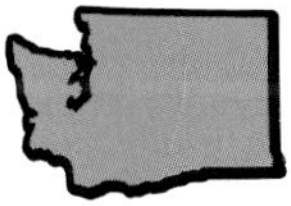

migration
winter

SAW IT!

STAN'S COOL STUFF

Early to **migrate** south into Washington and late to leave in spring. Eats mainly seeds but will eat fruit in fall and winter. Spends most of the time on the ground. Raises crown feathers while fighting with other sparrows.

Fox Sparrow

Look for the rusty-brown streaks on the chest

What to look for:
rusty-red bird with a heavily streaked chest, a solid rusty-red tail, and sooty gray head and back

Where you'll find them:
on the ground in shrubby areas, backyards, open fields, and under feeders

Calls and songs:
gives a series of notes lasting 2–3 seconds, often singing from a hidden perch in a shrub

On the move:
usually alone or in small groups; scratches the ground with both feet, like a chicken, to find food

What they eat:
seeds and insects; comes to ground feeders

Nest:
cup; on the ground in brush and along forest edges

Eggs, chicks, and childcare:
2–4 pale-green eggs with reddish marks; Mom **incubates** the eggs; Mom and Dad feed the kids

Spends the winter:
in western coastal US and southwestern states

REAL QUICK

Size
7"

Nest
CUP

Feeder
GROUND

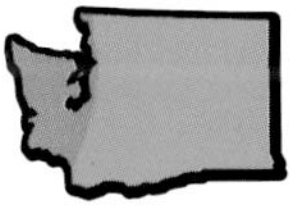

summer
winter

SAW ✓ **IT!**

STAN'S COOL STUFF

This is one of the largest sparrows. The name "Sparrow" comes from a very old word that means "flutterer." The name "Fox" was given for its rusty-red color. It has several color variations, including the Sooty and and the Slate-colored.

Horned Lark

Look for the black necklace

What to look for:
overall brown with black bib (necklace) and yellow chin

Where you'll find them:
on the ground in open **habitats**, fields, and along roads

Calls and songs:
a thin and delicate song followed by tinkling notes

On the move:
usually in small to large groups

What they eat:
seeds and insects

Nest:
well hidden on ground

Eggs, chicks, and childcare:
3–4 gray eggs with brown marks; Mom **incubates** the eggs; Mom and Dad feed the kids

Spends the winter:
in parts of southwestern states, Mexico, Central and South America; some stay in Washington

REAL QUICK

Size
7–8"

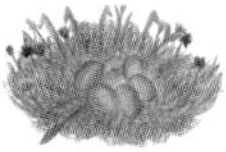

Nest
GROUND

Feeder
NONE

year-round
winter

SAW IT!

STAN'S COOL STUFF

A bird that thrives in a range of elevations, from sea level up to 13,000 feet. Often seen feeding along roads and then flying away to an open area as cars pass. Moves around a lot in winter.

Brown-headed Cowbird

Look for the pointed gray bill

What to look for:
brown bird with a sharp, pointed gray bill

Where you'll find them:
forest edges, open fields, farmlands, and backyards

Calls and songs:
sings a low, gurgling song that sounds like water moving; cowbird young are raised by other bird parents, but they still end up singing and calling like their own parents, without ever hearing them

On the move:
Mom flies quietly to another bird's nest, swiftly lays an egg, then flies quickly away

What they eat:
insects and seeds; visits seed feeders

Nest:
doesn't nest; lays eggs in the nests of other birds

Eggs, chicks, and childcare:
white eggs with brown marks; the **host** bird **incubates** any number of cowbird eggs in her nest and feeds the cowbird young along with her own

Spends the winter:
in southwestern states; some don't **migrate**

REAL QUICK

Size
7½"

Nest
NONE

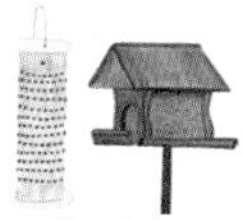

Feeder
TUBE OR HOPPER

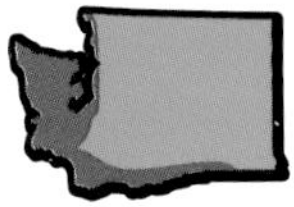

SAW IT!

STAN'S COOL STUFF

Cowbirds are **brood parasites**, meaning they don't nest or raise their own families. Instead, they lay their eggs in other birds' nests, leaving the host birds to raise their young. Cowbirds have laid their eggs in the nests of more than 200 other bird species.

Cedar Waxwing

Look for the black mask

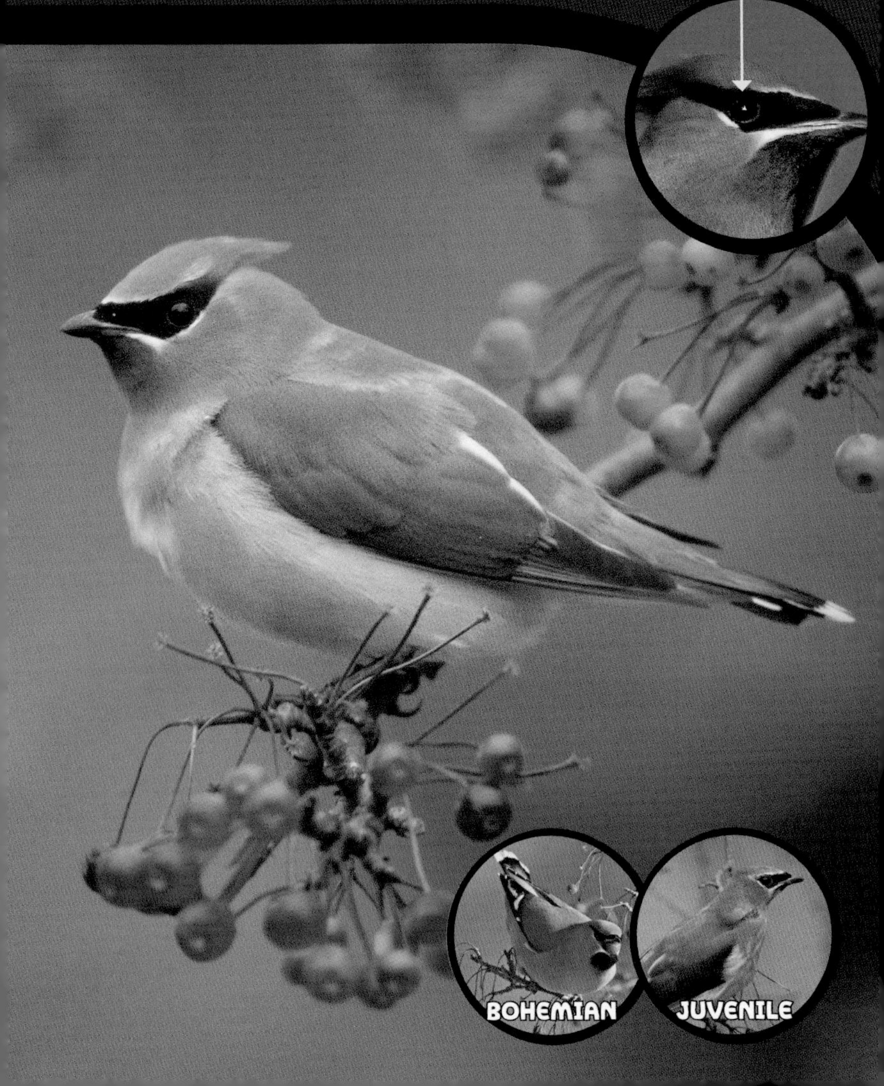

What to look for:
sleek bird with a pointed crest, black mask, light yellow belly, and waxy-looking red wing tips; tail has a bold yellow tip; **juvenile** lacks red wing tips

Where you'll find them:
treetops, forest edges, in trees with fruit

Calls and songs:
constantly makes a high-pitched "sreee" whistling sound while it's perched or in flight

On the move:
flies in **flocks** of 5–100 birds; moves from area to area, looking for berries

What they eat:
berry-like cedar cones, fruit, seeds and insects

Nest:
cup; Mom and Dad construct it together

Eggs, chicks, and childcare:
4–6 pale-blue eggs with brown marks; Mom sits on the eggs; Mom and Dad feed the little ones

Spends the winter:
in Washington; moves around to find food

REAL QUICK

Size
7½"

Nest
CUP

Feeder
NONE

year-round

SAW IT!

STAN'S COOL STUFF

The waxwing is named for its waxy-looking red wing tips and for the cedar's small, blueberry-like cones that it likes to eat. Before berries are abundant, it eats bugs. The young obtain the mask after their first year of life and red wing tips after their second year.

Black-headed Grosbeak

Look for the white eyebrows

pg. 191

What to look for:
yellowish-brown bird with a lighter breast and belly, bold white eyebrows, a large two-toned bill, and yellow wing linings (seen in flight)

Where you'll find them:
a wide variety of **habitats,** mostly in foothills and lower elevations

Calls and songs:
both males and females sing a rich song, similar to American Robins

On the move:
quick flight

What they eat:
seeds, insects, and fruit; visits seed feeders

Nest:
cup; Mom builds it

Eggs, chicks, and childcare:
3–4 pale-green-or-bluish eggs with brown marks; Mom and Dad sit on the eggs and feed the kids

Spends the winter:
in Mexico, Central America, and South America

REAL QUICK

Size
8"

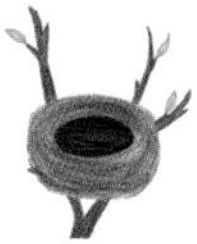

Nest
CUP

Feeder
HOPPER

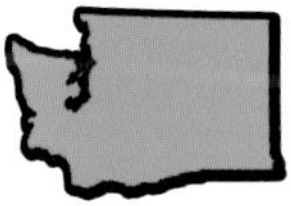

summer

SAW IT!

STAN'S COOL STUFF

Both the male and female sing and defend their territory. The large bill is used to crush seeds and also hard-bodied insects, such as beetles. Monarch butterflies are poisonous to most birds, but Black-headed Grosbeaks can eat them without getting sick.

Red-winged Blackbird

Look for the white eyebrows

What to look for:
heavily streaked with a pointed brown bill and white (sometimes yellow) eyebrows

Where you'll find them:
around marshes, wetlands, lakes, and rivers

Calls and songs:
male sings and repeats **calls** from cattail tops and the surrounding **vegetation**

On the move:
flocks with as many as 10,000 birds gather in autumn, often with other blackbirds

What they eat:
seeds in spring and autumn, insects in summer; visits seed and **suet** feeders

Nest:
cup; in a thick stand of cattails over shallow water

Eggs, chicks, and childcare:
3–4 speckled bluish-green eggs; Mom does all the **incubating**, but both parents feed the babies

Spends the winter:
in Washington; moves around to find food

REAL QUICK

Size
$8^1/_2$"

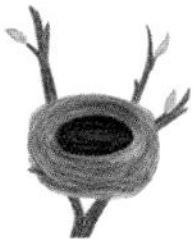

Nest
CUP

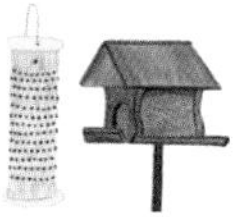

Feeder
TUBE OR HOPPER

year-round

SAW IT!

STAN'S COOL STUFF

During autumn and winter, thousands of these birds gather in farm fields, wetlands, and marshes. Come spring, males sing to defend territories and show off their wing patches (**epaulets**) to the females. Later, males can be aggressive when defending their nests.

Yellow-headed Blackbird

Look for the dull yellow head

pg. 27

What to look for:
brown bird with a dull yellow head and chest

Where you'll find them:
around marshes, wetlands, and lakes

Calls and songs:
usually heard before it is seen; gives a low, raspy, metallic-sounding **call**

On the move:
migrates in big **flocks** of up to 200 blackbirds; flocks of mainly males return in early April before the females

What they eat:
insects and seeds; comes to ground feeders

Nest:
cup in a deep-water marsh, in a large **colony** with 20–100 other nests

Eggs, chicks, and childcare:
3–5 speckled greenish-white eggs; Mom **incubates** the eggs and feeds the chicks

Spends the winter:
in southwestern states and Mexico

REAL QUICK

Size
9–11"

Nest
CUP

Feeder
GROUND

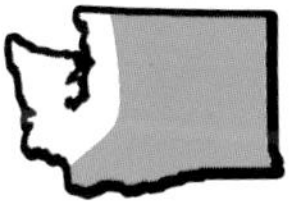

summer

SAW IT!

STAN'S COOL STUFF

The male performs a mating **display** in flight and when perched. He displays in flight with his head drooped, and his feet and tail pointing down. When perched, he throws his head back and calls. The young stay hidden for up to three weeks before starting to fly.

American Kestrel

Look for the black lines on the face

What to look for:
rusty back, blue-gray wings, spotted chest, two black lines on the face, a wide black band on the tip of tail; female has rusty wings, dark tail bands

Where you'll find them:
open fields, prairies, farm fields, along highways

Calls and songs:
loud series of high-pitched "klee-klee-klee" **calls**

On the move:
hovers in midair near roads, then dives for **prey**; pumps tail up and down after landing on a perch

What they eat:
bugs (especially grasshoppers), small animals, birds, and reptiles

Nest:
cavity in a tree or wooden nest box; doesn't add nesting material

Eggs, chicks, and childcare:
4–5 white eggs with brown marks; parents take turns sitting on the eggs and feeding the babies

Spends the winter:
in Washington; moves around in winter to find food

REAL QUICK

Size
9–11"

Nest
CAVITY

Feeder
NONE

year-round
winter

SAW IT!

STAN'S COOL STUFF

The kestrel is a small falcon that perches nearly upright. The male and female have different markings—this is unusual for a **raptor**. It can see **ultraviolet light**. That ability helps it find mice and other prey by their urine, which glows bright yellow in ultraviolet light.

Killdeer

Look for the two black neck bands

What to look for:
brown back, white belly, and two black bands around the neck like a **necklace**; a bold reddish-orange rump, visible in flight

Where you'll find them:
open country, vacant fields, along railroad tracks, driveways, gravel pits, and wetland edges

Calls and songs:
gives a very loud and distinctive "kill-deer" **call**

On the move:
fakes a broken wing to draw intruders away from the nest, and then takes flight once the nest is safe

What they eat:
loves bugs; also eats worms and snails

Nest:
ground nest; Dad makes just a slight depression in gravel, often very hard to see

Eggs, chicks, and childcare:
3–5 tan eggs with brown marks; Dad and Mom **incubate** the eggs and lead the **hatchlings** to food

Spends the winter:
in southwestern states, Mexico, and Central America

REAL QUICK

Size
11"

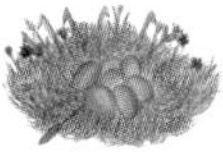

Nest
GROUND

Feeder
NONE

year-round
summer

SAW ✓ IT!

STAN'S COOL STUFF

Scientists group the Killdeer in the family of shorebirds, but you're more likely to spot one along railroad tracks, around farms, and in other dry **habitats** than you are at the lakeshore. It's the only shorebird with two black neck bands. They **migrate** in small **flocks**.

Northern Flicker

Look for the red mustache

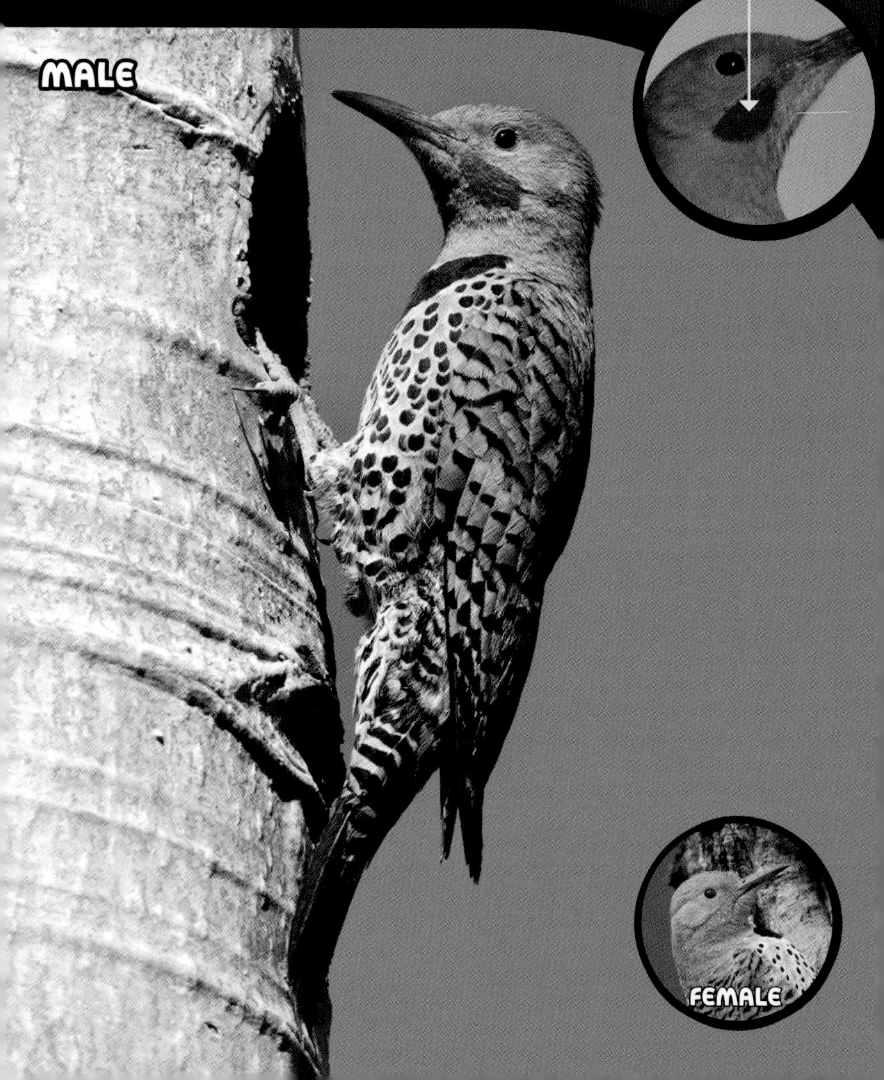

What to look for:
male is brown-and-black with a red mustache, black **necklace**, and speckled chest; female lacks the red mustache

Where you'll find them:
forests, small woods, backyards, and parks

Calls and songs:
gives a loud "wacka-wacka" **call**

On the move:
flies in a deep, exaggerated up-and-down pattern, flashing yellow under its wings and tail

What they eat:
insects (especially ants and beetles); known to eat the eggs of other birds; visits **suet** feeders

Nest:
cavity in a tree or in a nest box that is stuffed with sawdust; often reuses an old nest several times

Eggs, chicks, and childcare:
5–8 white eggs; Mom and Dad **incubate** the eggs and feed the baby woodpeckers

Spends the winter:
in Washington

REAL QUICK

Size
12"

Nest
CAVITY

Feeder
SUET

year-round

SAW ☑ IT!

STAN'S COOL STUFF

The Northern Flicker is the only woodpecker to regularly feed on the ground. The male often picks the nest site, usually a natural cavity in a tree. Both parents will pitch in to dig as needed, taking as many as 12 days to finish **excavating** a hole.

Mourning Dove

Look for the small round head

What to look for:
brown-to-gray bird with shiny, **iridescent** pink and greenish-blue on the neck, a gray patch on the head, and black spots on the wings and tail

Where you'll find them:
around your seed and ground feeders, open fields

Calls and songs:
known for its soft, sad (mournful) cooing

On the move:
wind rushes through its wing feathers during takeoff and flight, creating a whistling sound

What they eat:
seeds; visits ground and seed feeders

Nest:
flimsy platform in a tree, made with twigs; often falls apart in a storm or during high winds

Eggs, chicks, and childcare:
2 white eggs; parents **incubate** the eggs and feed a **regurgitated** liquid to their young for the first few days of life

Spends the winter:
in southwestern states; many don't **migrate**

REAL QUICK

Size
12"

Nest
PLATFORM

Feeder
GROUND

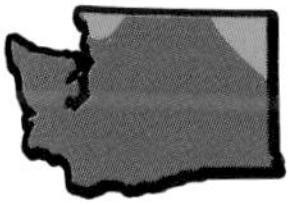

year-round
summer

SAW IT!

STAN'S COOL STUFF

The dove is a ground feeder that bobs its head as it walks. It's one of the few birds that drinks without lifting its head, like the Rock Pigeon (pg. 161). Parents regurgitate a liquid, called **crop-milk**, to feed to their young (**squab**) during their first few days of life.

Pied-billed Grebe

Look for the black ring around the bill

What to look for:
small brown waterbird with a black ring on a thick ivory bill and a puffy white patch under the tail; winter **plumage** has a brown bill

Where you'll find them:
wetlands, ponds, and lakes

Calls and songs:
a rhythmic series of very loud whooping **calls**

On the move:
often dives while swimming, entirely submerging itself to catch food; it can reappear on the surface far from where it went under

What they eat:
crayfish, aquatic insects, and fish

Nest:
ground nest floating in water

Eggs, chicks, and childcare:
5–7 bluish-white eggs; Mom and Dad sit on the eggs and tend to the baby grebes

Spends the winter:
in southwestern states, Mexico, and Central America

REAL QUICK

Size
12–14"

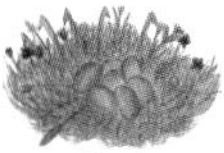

Nest
GROUND

Feeder
NONE

year-round
summer

SAW IT!

STAN'S COOL STUFF

The grebe is well suited to aquatic life. It has short wings, lobed toes, and legs set close to the rear of its body, making it awkward on land. When it's been disturbed, it compresses its feathers to get the air out, and then sinks underwater like a submarine.

Green-winged Teal

Look for the dark green patch on the head

What to look for:

male has a gray body, a chestnut head with a dark green patch from the eyes to the neck, a green patch on the wings (**speculum**), and a yellow tail; female is light-brown with black spots and a green speculum

Where you'll find them:

small lakes, ponds, and quiet streams

Calls and songs:

females have a weak quack; males produce a strong whistle

On the move:

extremely fast flyer with constant quick wing-beats; green speculum is seen in flight

What they eat:

aquatic plants and insects

Nest:

ground; Mom builds it

Eggs, chicks, and childcare:

8–10 cream-white eggs; Mom **incubates** the eggs; Mom teaches the chicks to feed

Spends the winter:

in Washington

REAL QUICK

Size
14–15"

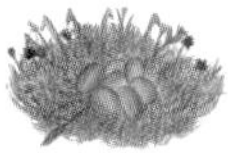

Nest
GROUND

Feeder
NONE

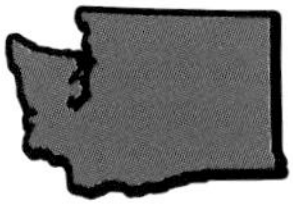

year-round

SAW IT!

STAN'S COOL STUFF

These are the smallest of the teals. During winter they form large **flocks** and move around to find food. They are usually found on shallow ponds and lakes. Fast flyers, they can reach 70 miles per hour in level flight.

Cinnamon Teal

Look for the deep red eyes

What to look for:
cinnamon head, neck, and belly and a light-brown back; dark-gray bill and deep-red eyes; winter male is overall brown with a red tinge; female is overall brown with a pale-brown head, long shovel-like bill, and green patch on wings

Where you'll find them:
shallow ponds and lakes

Calls and songs:
males give a snoring, rattling **call**; females give a high-pitched typical quack

On the move:
fast, direct flight with constant wing flaps

What they eat:
aquatic plants and insects, seeds

Nest:
ground; Mom builds it

Eggs, chicks, and childcare:
7–12 pinkish-white eggs; Mom **incubates** the eggs and teaches the chicks to feed

Spends the winter:
in southwestern states and Mexico

REAL QUICK

Size
15–17"

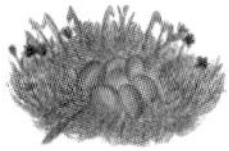

Nest
GROUND

Feeder
NONE

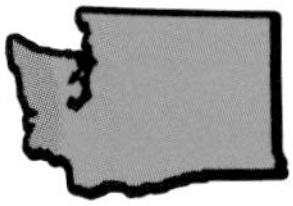

summer
migration

SAW IT!

STAN'S COOL STUFF

Males are an amazing rich red color but **molt** to a brown coat of feathers, very similar to females, after breeding season. Cinnamon Teal have a much longer and wider bill than other teal species. Often a very quiet bird, unlike many other duck species.

Wood Duck

Look for the bold white eye-ring

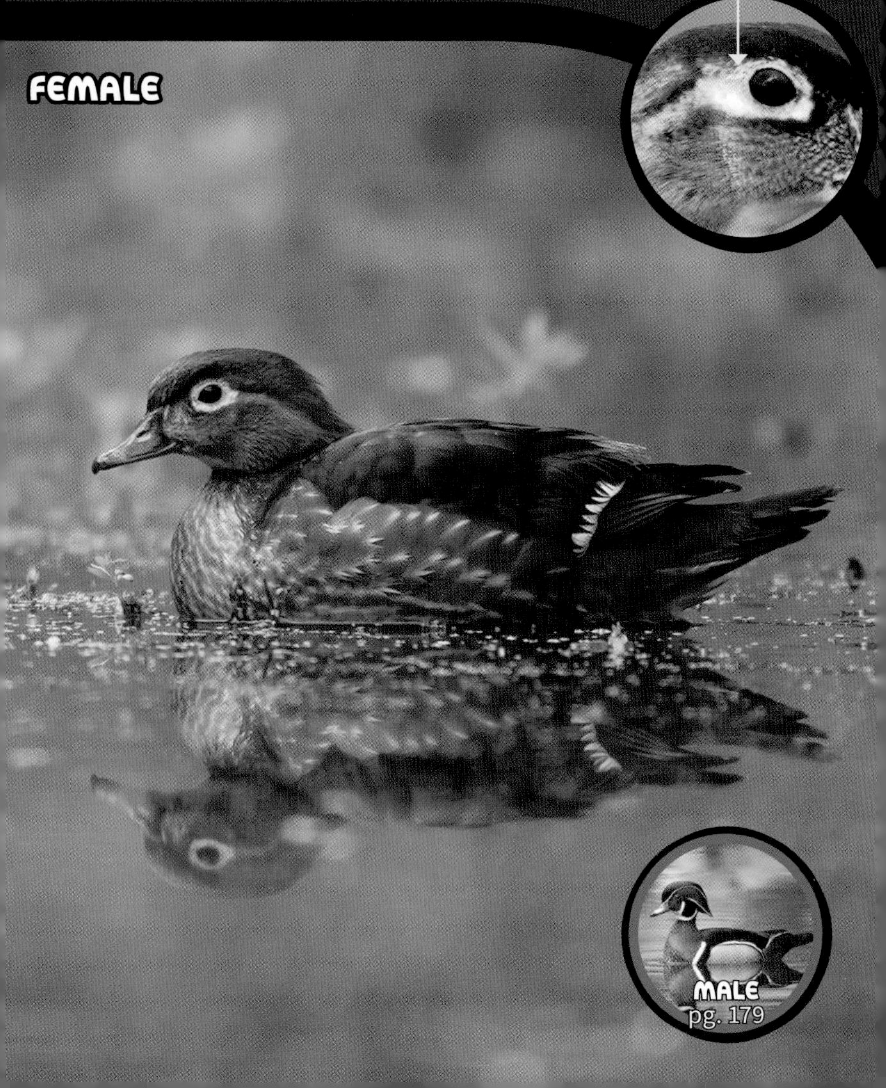

FEMALE

MALE

pg. 179

What to look for:
brown with a bold white eye-ring; crest on head and blue wing patch (**speculum**) are harder to see

Where you'll find them:
quiet, shallow ponds; deep in the woods and up on tree branches

Calls and songs:
female **calls** "oo-eek, oo-eek" when startled and at takeoff; male calls a zipper-like "zeeeet"

On the move:
blasts off from the water with loud calls and noisy wings; flies quickly through forest; enters cavity nest from full flight; small, tight group flights

What they eat:
aquatic insects, plants, and seeds

Nest:
cavity; adds a lining of soft, downy feathers in an old woodpecker hole or a nest box

Eggs, chicks, and childcare:
10–15 creamy-white eggs; only Mom **incubates** the eggs and shows the kids how to feed

Spends the winter:
in southwestern states; some don't **migrate**

REAL QUICK

Size
17–20"

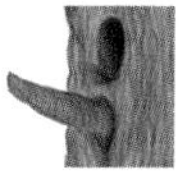

Nest
CAVITY

Feeder
NONE

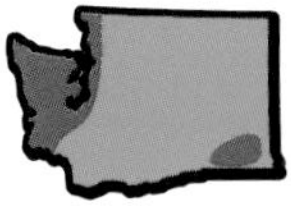

year-round
summer

SAW IT!

STAN'S COOL STUFF

This is a small dabbling duck. The female lays some eggs in a neighbor's nest (egg dumping), sometimes resulting in 20 or more eggs in a nest! The young stay in the nest for a day, then jump from as high as 60 feet to the ground or water and follow Mom.

Mallard

Look for the orange-and-black bill

What to look for:
overall brown duck with an orange-and-black bill, a white tail, and a blue-and-white wing mark (**speculum**), seen best in flight

Where you'll find them:
lakes and ponds, rivers and streams, and maybe even your backyard

Calls and songs:
the sound a duck makes is based on the female Mallard's classic quack; the male doesn't quack

On the move:
sometimes in huge **flocks** with hundreds of ducks; mostly in small flocks of 6–10, especially in spring

What they eat:
seeds, aquatic plants, and insects; visits ground feeders offering corn

Nest:
ground nest; Mom builds it from plants nearby

Eggs, chicks, and childcare:
7–10 greenish-to-whitish eggs; Mom **incubates** the eggs and leads the young to food

Spends the winter:
in Washington

REAL QUICK

Size
19–21"

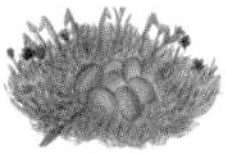

Nest
GROUND

Feeder
GROUND

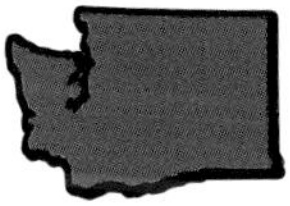

year-round

SAW IT!

STAN'S COOL STUFF

Mallards are found in most countries around the world. Males are called drakes, and females are called hens. This is one of the only duck species that can take off vertically. Only the female gives the loud and typical "quack, quack, quack" call.

Northern Shoveler

Look for the large, shovel-like bill

pg. 183

What to look for:
brown duck with black speckles, green wing mark (**speculum**), and a super-large, spoon-shaped bill

Where you'll find them:
shallow wetlands, ponds, and small lakes

Calls and songs:
female gives a classic quack; male gives a crazy-sounding combination of popping and quacking, calling, "puk-puk, puk-puk, puk-puk"

On the move:
swims in tight circles, stirring up insects to eat; small **flocks** of 5–10 birds swim with bills pointing toward the water; flocks fly in tight formation

What they eat:
enjoys aquatic insects; likes plants, too

Nest:
ground nest; Mom forms plant material into a circle

Eggs, chicks, and childcare:
9–12 olive-colored eggs; Mom sits on the eggs and leads her little shovelers to food

Spends the winter:
in southwestern states, Mexico, and Central America; some don't **migrate**

REAL QUICK

Size
19–21"

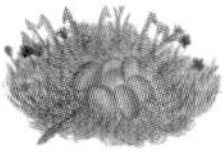

Nest
GROUND

Feeder
NONE

year-round
summer

SAW IT!

STAN'S COOL STUFF

The Northern Shoveler is a medium-sized duck. It is the only shoveler species found in North America. The name "Shoveler" refers to its peculiar, shovel-like bill. It feeds by using its bill to sift tiny aquatic insects and plants floating on the water's surface.

Northern Harrier

Look for the large white rump patch

MALE
pg. 167

What to look for:
mostly brown with tan undersides and white rump patch

Where you'll find them:
open fields, swamps, cattail marshes, and prairies

Calls and songs:
usually silent; fast series of "kek" notes lasting 1–2 seconds

On the move:
low to ground, following contour of the land

What they eat:
small animals, snakes, and large bugs

Nest:
on ground, usually under dense shrub

Eggs, chicks, and childcare:
4–8 bluish-white eggs; Mom sits on the eggs; both parents provide for the youngsters

Spends the winter:
in Washington; moves around in winter

REAL QUICK

Size
18–22"

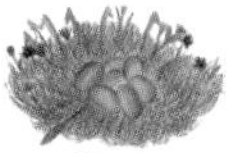

Nest
GROUND

Feeder
NONE

year-round
summer

SAW IT!

STAN'S COOL STUFF

Also called Marsh Hawk, one of the few species of **raptor** where males and females don't look alike. It has facial disks like an owl, but it is a type of hawk. It uses its good sense of hearing to find prey when flying close to the ground

Rough-legged Hawk

Look for the wide dark belly band

What to look for:
a medium-sized hawk with a wide dark-brown belly band

Where you'll find them:
open areas

Calls and songs:
alarm **call** sounds like a cat-like mew lasting 1–2 seconds

On the move:
up high in air, perches at top of trees on thin branches

What they eat:
small animals, snakes, and large bugs

Nest:
usually on a cliff face

Eggs, chicks, and childcare:
2–6 white eggs; parents sit on the eggs and provide for the youngsters

Spends the winter:
in Washington

REAL QUICK

Size
18–23"

Nest
PLATFORM

Feeder
NONE

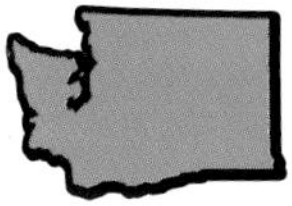

winter

SAW IT!

STAN'S COOL STUFF

It nests up in the Arctic and comes to Washington in winter. There are two forms of this bird, called **morphs**: light and dark. The name comes from its heavily feathered legs and feet. It is one of only a few hawks with feathers on legs and feet.

Red-tailed Hawk

Look for the rusty-red tail

What to look for:

plumage varies, but it's often brown with a white chest, brown belly band, and a rusty-red tail

Where you'll find them:

just about anywhere; open country, where it flies over open fields and roadsides; cities, where it perches on freeway light posts, fences, and trees

Calls and songs:

gives a high-pitched scream that trails off

On the move:

hunts in flight, flying in circles as it searches for **prey**

What they eat:

mice and other mammals, birds, snakes, large bugs

Nest:

large platform made of sticks, lined with materials such as evergreen needles; often in a large tree

Eggs, chicks, and childcare:

2–3 white eggs, sometimes speckled; parents sit on the eggs and provide for the youngsters

Spends the winter:

in Washington

REAL QUICK

Size
19–23"

Nest
PLATFORM

Feeder
NONE

year-round

SAW IT!

STAN'S COOL STUFF

This **raptor** is a large hawk with a wide variety of colors from bird to bird, ranging from chocolate to nearly all white. The red color of the tail develops in the second year of life and usually is best seen from above. It returns to the same nest site each year.

Barred Owl

Look for the dark eyes

What to look for:
brown-to-gray owl with dark-brown eyes, dark horizontal bars on upper chest, vertical streaks on the lower chest and belly, yellow bill and feet

Where you'll find them:
likes dense woodlands

Calls and songs:
gives calls of 6–8 hoots, sounding something like "who-who-who-cooks-for-you"

On the move:
a smooth and silent flight, gliding on flat, outstretched wings; often hunts during the day, perching and watching for mice and other **prey**

What they eat:
small mammals, birds, fish, reptiles, amphibians

Nest:
natural cavity in a tree or uses a nest box with a large entrance hole; doesn't add nesting material

Eggs, chicks, and childcare:
2–3 white eggs; Mom sits on the eggs; Mom and Dad attend to the babies

Spends the winter:
doesn't **migrate**; stays in Washington year-round

REAL QUICK

Size
20–24"

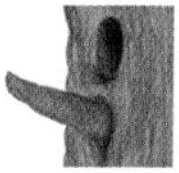

Nest
CAVITY

Feeder
NONE

year-round

SAW IT!

STAN'S COOL STUFF

Nearly identical to the Northern Spotted Owl. It's a chunky bird with a large head. It fishes by hovering over water, and then reaches down to grab one. The young stay with their parents for up to four months after fledging.

Northern Pintail

Look for the extremely long tail

What to look for:
male has a brown head, white neck, a gray bill and body, and an extremely long and narrow black tail; winter male has a paler head and lacks the long tail feathers; female has a mottled brown body with a paler head and neck, a gray bill, and a long tail

Where you'll find them:
freshwater lakes and ponds

Calls and songs:
male gives a wheezy train-like whistle **call;** female gives a stuttering quack that is similar to female mallards

On the move:
fast, straight flight up to 60 miles per hour

What they eat:
aquatic plants and insects, seeds

Nest:
ground; Mom builds

Eggs, chicks, and childcare:
6–9 olive-green egg; Mom **incubates** the eggs; Mom teaches young to feed

Spends the winter:
in Washington

REAL QUICK

Size
20–25"

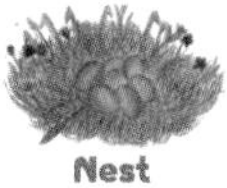

Nest
GROUND

Feeder
NONE

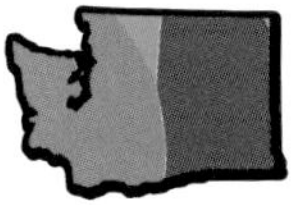

year-round
summer
winter

SAW IT!

STAN'S COOL STUFF

Found around the world in the Northern Hemisphere, these ducks nest on the ground, often far from water, making them vulnerable to predators. Once one of the most common ducks in North America, populations have declined due to disease and hunting.

Great Horned Owl

Look for the feather tufts on the head

What to look for:
"eared" owl with large yellow eyes, a V-shaped white marking, and horizontal bars on the chest

Where you'll find them:
just about any **habitat** throughout Washington

Calls and songs:
calls a familiar "hoo-hoo-hoo-hoooo"

On the move:
flies silently on big wings that stretch out to 4 feet across; takes a few quick flaps, and then glides

What they eat:
small-to-medium mammals, birds (especially ducks), snakes, and insects

Nest:
no nest; takes over the nest of another bird or uses a broken tree stump or other semi-cavity

Eggs, chicks, and childcare:
nesting in Washington typically starts in January, but it could be as early as December; 2–3 white eggs; Mom **incubates**; Dad and Mom both feed the **hatchlings**

Spends the winter:
doesn't **migrate;** usually hangs around the same area year after year

REAL QUICK

Size
21–25"

Nest
NONE

Feeder
NONE

year-round

SAW IT!

STAN'S COOL STUFF

The "**horns**" of the Great Horned are feather tufts, not ears. Its eyelids close from the top down, like ours. It has fabulous hearing and can hear a mouse moving under a deep pile of leaves. It's one of the few animals that will kill a skunk or a porcupine.

Golden Eagle

Look for the yellow around base of bill

What to look for:
dark brown with a golden-yellow head and **nape,** yellow around the base of the bill, and yellow feet

Where you'll find them:
open mountainous areas

Calls and songs:
usually silent; gives weak high-pitched whistle

On the move:
soaring on outstretched wings

What they eat:
mammals, birds, reptiles, and insects

Nest:
platform nest on a cliff; Mom and Dad team up to build it

Eggs, chicks, and childcare:
1–2 white eggs with brown marks; Mom and Dad sit on the eggs and bring in food for the kids

Spends the winter:
in Washington; moves around to find food

REAL QUICK

Size
30–40"

Nest
PLATFORM

Feeder
NONE

year-round
winter

SAW IT!

STAN'S COOL STUFF

The Golden Eagle is a large, powerful **raptor** that hunts for **prey** up to the size of a red fox while soaring or perched high on rocky cliffs. They use the same nest for many years. The name "Golden" comes from the gold-colored feathers on its neck.

Wild Turkey

Look for the bare blue-and-red head

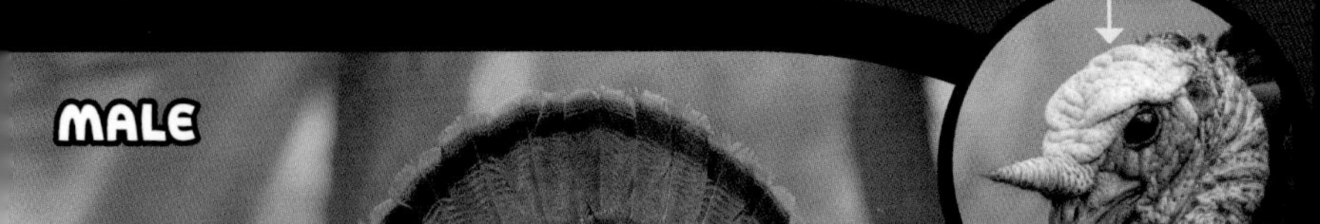

What to look for:
male is a funny-looking brown-and-bronze bird with a bare blue-and-red head, long thin beard, and a large fanning tail; female is thinner, duller, and often lacks a beard

Where you'll find them:
just about any **habitat**, from suburban yards to prairies and forests

Calls and songs:
a fast, descending "gobble-gobble-gobble-gobble" that's often heard before the bird is seen

On the move:
a strong flier that can approach 60 miles per hour; also able to fly straight up, and then away

What they eat:
insects, seeds, and fruit

Nest:
ground nest; Mom scrapes out a shallow depression and pads it with soft leaves

Eggs, chicks, and childcare:
10–12 whitish eggs with dull brown marks; Mom sits on the eggs and leads the babies to food

Spends the winter:
moves around Washington to find **cover** and food

REAL QUICK

Size
36–48"

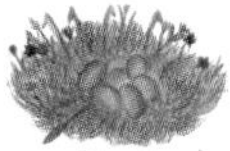

Nest
GROUND

Feeder
NONE

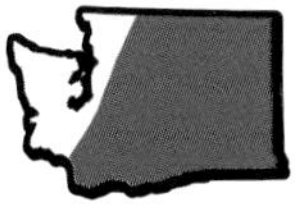

year-round

SAW IT!

STAN'S COOL STUFF

The turkey is the largest native game bird in Washington. It sees three times better than people, and it can hear sounds from a mile away. A male will lead a group of up to 20 females. The male's head and neck change color when **displaying** for females.

Ruby-crowned Kinglet

Look for the ruby crown

What to look for:
small, teardrop-shaped green-to-gray bird; two white wing bars and a white eye ring; hidden ruby crown

Where you'll find them:
thick shrubs low to the ground

Calls and songs:
a distinctive song that starts out soft and ends loud and on a higher note

On the move:
quickly flits from one low branch to another; rarely stays still

What they eat:
insects and berries; will come to peanut or **suet** feeders if no insects available

Nest:
pendulous; Mom builds it

Eggs, chicks, and childcare:
4–5 white eggs with brown marks; Mom **incubates** the eggs and Dad helps her feed the kids

Spends the winter:
in parts of Washington

REAL QUICK

Size
4"

Nest
PENDULOUS

Feeder
TUBE OR SUET

year-round
summer
winter

SAW IT!

STAN'S COOL STUFF

One of the smallest birds in Washington. The red (ruby) crown is often hidden until the bird is excited. Early spring migrant, often traveling in **flocks** with other birds. Constantly singing in spring during migration. Rarely stops while feeding and **migrating**.

Red-breasted Nuthatch

Look for the rusty-red chest

MALE

FEMALE

What to look for:
male has a black cap and eye line, gray back, and rusty-red chest and belly; female is similar, but with a gray cap and pale undersides

Where you'll find them:
mature **coniferous** forests, where it removes seeds from pine cones; hangs out near bird feeders

Calls and songs:
gives a funny series of nasal "yank-yank-yank" **calls,** sounding like the horn of a clown's car

On the move:
climbs down trees headfirst to find and eat the insects that other birds climbing up missed

What they eat:
insects, insect eggs, and seeds; will visit seed and **suet** feeders

Nest:
cavity; Dad and Mom **excavate** or move into an old woodpecker hole or a natural cavity

Eggs, chicks, and childcare:
5–6 white eggs with reddish-brown marks; Mom **incubates** the eggs, and Dad helps her feed the kids

Spends the winter:
in Washington; moves around to find food

REAL QUICK

Size
4½"

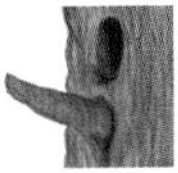

Nest
CAVITY

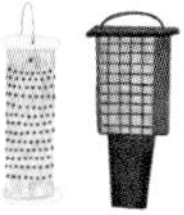

Feeder
TUBE OR SUET

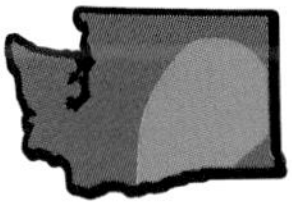

year-round
winter

SAW IT!

STAN'S COOL STUFF

The nuthatch grabs a seed from a feeder, wedges it into a crevice and pounds it a few times to crack it open. "Nuthatch" comes from a very old word, *nuthak*, which refers to its habit of hacking seeds. It's an irruptive **migrator**, common in some winters, rare in others.

Black-capped Chickadee

Look for the black cap

What to look for:
mostly gray bird with a black cap and throat patch, tan sides and belly, and a white chest

Where you'll find them:
nearly all **habitats**—just look around for this bird

Calls and songs:
calls "chika-dee-dee-dee-dee"; also gives a high-pitched, two-toned "fee-bee" **call** during spring; can have different calls in different regions

On the move:
flies short distances with short, fluttery wings

What they eat:
seeds, bugs, and fruit; visits seed and **suet** feeders

Nest:
excavates a cavity or uses a nest box; gathers mostly green moss for the nest and fur to line it

Eggs, chicks, and childcare:
5–7 white eggs with fine brown marks; Mom and Dad sit on the eggs and feed their **brood**

Spends the winter:
doesn't **migrate**; moves around to find food and shelter instead; must feed every day in winter and forages for food even during the worst snowstorms

REAL QUICK

Size
5"

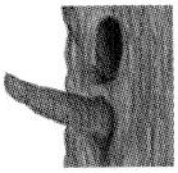

Nest
CAVITY

Feeder
TUBE OR SUET

year-round

SAW ✓ **IT!**

STAN'S COOL STUFF

You can attract this bird with a seed feeder or nest box. Usually it's the first to find a new feeder. It is easily tamed and hand-fed. Most of the diet comes from bird feeders, so it can be a common urban bird. It's often seen with nuthatches, woodpeckers, and other birds.

Mountain Chickadee

Look for the black line through the eyes

What to look for:
a gray bird with a black cap, chin, and line through the eyes, and white eyebrows

Where you'll find them:
coniferous forests and mountainous areas

Calls and songs:
a clear whistle that says its name, "chick-a-dee-dee"

On the move:
quick flaps to zip from tree to tree

What they eat:
seeds and bugs; visits seed and **suet** feeders

Nest:
excavates a cavity, or uses a nest box or old woodpecker cavity, and lines it with moss, hair, and feathers

Eggs, chicks, and childcare:
5–8 white eggs; parents take turns sitting on the eggs and feeding the young

Spends the winter:
in Washington; forms small social **flocks** with other chickadees, nuthatches, and others; often moves to lower elevations in winter

REAL QUICK

Size
5½"

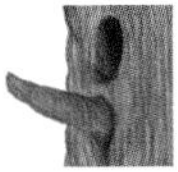

Nest
CAVITY

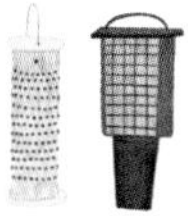

Feeder
TUBE OR SUET

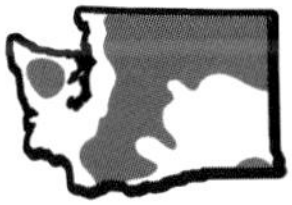

year-round

SAW IT!

STAN'S COOL STUFF

This is a very common bird in Washington. This bird feeds mainly on insects in warm months and seeds in winter. In summer, it is found only in pairs, while during winter they gather in large groups and join other species of birds to look for food and to stay safe.

White-breasted Nuthatch

Look for the white chest

MALE

FEMALE

What to look for:
male has a gray back with a white face, chest, and belly; a black cap and **nape** of neck; and a large white patch on the rump; female is similar except with a gray cap and nape

Where you'll find them:
woodlands, parks, backyards, and forest edges

Calls and songs:
a characteristic spring **call**, "whi-whi-whi-whi," given during February and March

On the move:
climbs down tree trunks headfirst, looking for hidden insects; quick, short flights from tree to tree

What they eat:
insects, insect eggs, and seeds; visits seed and **suet** feeders

Nest:
cavity; Mom and Dad build a nest in an empty woodpecker hole or a natural cavity

Eggs, chicks, and childcare:
5–7 white eggs with brown marks; Mom sits on the eggs; Mom and Dad feed the little ones

Spends the winter:
doesn't **migrate;** stays in Washington

REAL QUICK

Size
5–6"

Nest
CAVITY

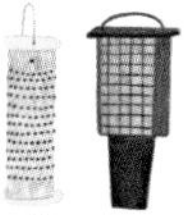

Feeder
TUBE OR SUET

year-round

SAW IT!

STAN'S COOL STUFF

The White-breasted Nuthatch has an extra-long hind toe claw, called a nail, on each foot, giving it the ability to cling to trees and climb down headfirst. Pairs stay together all year and defend their territory.

Yellow-rumped Warbler

Look for the bright yellow patches

What to look for:
gray with black streaks on the chest and yellow patches on head, flanks, and rump; female is duller gray; first-winter **juvenile** is similar to the female

Where you'll find them:
can be seen in any **habitat** during **migration;** seems to prefer **deciduous** forests and forest edges

Calls and songs:
sings a wonderful song in spring; **calls** a single robust "chip," heard mostly during migration

On the move:
quickly moves among trees and from the ground to trees; flits around upper branches of tall trees

What they eat:
insects and berries; visits **suet** feeders in spring

Nest:
cup; Mom builds the nest on her own in forests

Eggs, chicks, and childcare:
4–5 white eggs with brown marks; Mom sits on the eggs; Mom and Dad feed the young

Spends the winter:
in southwestern states, Mexico, and Central America; doesn't migrate in western Washington

REAL QUICK

Size
5-6"

Nest
CUP

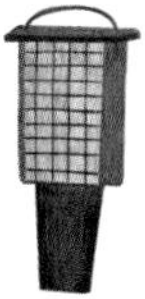

Feeder
SUET

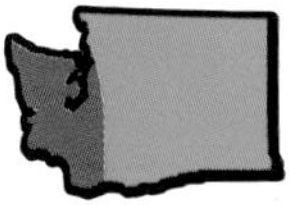

year-round
summer

SAW ✓ IT!

STAN'S COOL STUFF

West Coast birds have a yellow throat and are called Audubon's; birds with white throat in other parts of the US are called Myrtle. Both are called Yellow-rumped Warbler. It is one of the last warblers to arrive in winter and one of the first to leave in spring.

Dark-eyed Junco

Look for the pink bill

What to look for:
plump bird with a gray-to-charcoal chest, head, and back; a white belly; and a tiny pink bill

Where you'll find them:
on the ground in small **flocks** with other juncos and sparrows

Calls and songs:
a beautiful, loud, musical **trill** lasting 2–3 seconds

On the move:
outermost tail feathers are white and appear as a white V during flight

What they eat:
seeds (scarfs down many weed seeds) and insects; visits ground and seed feeders

Nest:
cup on the ground in a wide variety of **habitats;** female chooses a well-hidden nest site

Eggs, chicks, and childcare:
3–5 white eggs with reddish-brown marks; Mom **incubates** the eggs; Dad and Mom feed the babies

Spends the winter:
in much of Washington; moves around to find food

REAL QUICK

Size
5½"

Nest
CUP

Feeder
GROUND

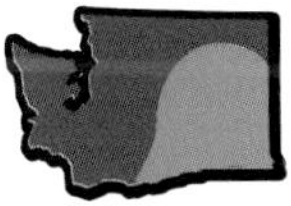

year-round
winter

SAW IT!

STAN'S COOL STUFF

The junco is one of our most common winter birds. Usually just the females are seen here because they **migrate** farther south. This round, dark-eyed bird uses both feet at the same time to "**double-scratch**" the ground, exposing seeds and insects to eat.

American Dipper

Look for the lighter-colored head

What to look for:
dark gray to black overall, with a head that is slightly lighter in color, a short upturned tail, and dark eyes and bill

Where you'll find them:
fast-running streams and rivers

Calls and songs:
a clear, sweet song with notes that repeat

On the move:
has the ability to fly directly into the air from underwater

What they eat:
aquatic insects, small fish, and **crustaceans**

Nest:
covered ground nest with the entrance near the bottom; nests are found on cliffs or even behind waterfalls

Eggs, chicks, and childcare:
3–5 white eggs; Mom sits on the eggs; both parents feed the young

Spends the winter:
in Washington; moves around to find open water in winter

REAL QUICK

Size
7½"

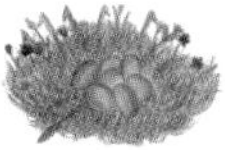

Nest
GROUND

Feeder
NONE

year-round

SAW IT!

STAN'S COOL STUFF

This interesting bird plunges headfirst into fast-moving streams to hunt aquatic insects. It swims underwater and even walks across the bottom of the stream. Then it returns to the water's surface to eat, often smashing the insect against a rock before eating it.

Townsend's Solitaire

Look for the white eye ring

What to look for:
looks like an all-gray robin; wings slightly darker than the body, long tail, and short dark bill; dark eyes with prominent white ring around each eye

Where you'll find them:
pine and spruce forests

Calls and songs:
a rich **warble** that sounds similar to the House Finch

On the move:
flies directly to top of tree, perches upright and sings

What they eat:
insects and fruit

Nest:
cup; Mom builds it

Eggs, chicks, and childcare:
3–5 blue, green, gray, or white eggs with brown marks; Mom sits on the eggs; Mom and Dad feed the babies

Spends the winter:
in Washington; moves around to find food in winter

REAL QUICK

Size
8½"

Nest
CUP

Feeder
NONE

year-round
winter

SAW IT!

STAN'S COOL STUFF

Spends summer in higher elevations and moves lower during the winter. If they find a good food source, they hang around all winter. They nest in dirt banks along rivers and roads. They often fly quickly from their perch to grab insects that are flying by.

American Robin

Look for the rusty-red breast

What to look for:
male has a black head and a rich, rusty-red breast; female is duller with a gray head and lighter breast

Where you'll find them:
loves to hop on lawns in search of worms

Calls and songs:
chips and chirps; sings all night in spring; studies report that city robins sing louder than country robins so they can be heard over traffic and noise

On the move:
found all over the US in an amazing range of **habitats,** from sea level to mountaintops

What they eat:
insects, fruit, and berries, as well as earthworms

Nest:
cup; weaves plant materials and uses mud to plaster the nest to a sheltered location

Eggs, chicks, and childcare:
4–7 pale-blue eggs; Mom sits on the eggs; Mom and Dad feed the baby robins

Spends the winter:
in Washington; moves around to find food

REAL QUICK

Size
9–11"

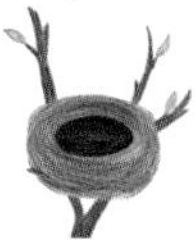

Nest
CUP

Feeder
NONE

year-round

SAW IT!

STAN'S COOL STUFF

When a robin walks across your lawn and turns its head to the side, it isn't listening for worms—it is looking for them. Because its eyes are on the sides of its head, a robin must focus its sight out of one eye to see the moving dirt caused by a worm.

California Quail

Look for the plume on the forehead

MALE

FEMALE

What to look for:
plump gray bird with a black face and chin with bold white markings, a pale brown forehead with a prominent teardrop-shaped plume, and a "scaled" appearance on the belly that can be light brown to white; female is similar to the male but lacks the black-and-white face and chin markings

Where you'll find them:
open fields, farm areas, and sagebrush

Calls and songs:
A single **call** note given 10 or more times in a row

On the move:
usually walking or running; will fly when scared

What they eat:
seeds, leaves, insects; visits ground feeders

Nest:
ground; Mom builds

Eggs, chicks, and childcare:
12–16 white eggs with brown marks; Mom **incubates** the eggs and Dad helps her teach the young to feed

Spends the winter:
in Washington

REAL QUICK

Size
10"

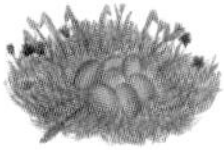

Nest
GROUND

Feeder
GROUND

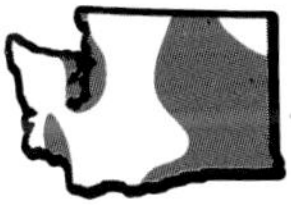

year-round

SAW IT!

STAN'S COOL STUFF

Quail live on the ground during the day and fly only when forced. They roost (rest or sleep) in trees at night. During summer they spend time in small groups (called coveys), but in winter they can be in groups of up to 100. Their range is expanding in Washington.

Canada Jay

Look for the white forehead

What to look for:
large gray bird with a white forehead and **nape** of neck, short black bill, and dark eyes

Where you'll find them:
coniferous forest above 8,000 feet elevation

Calls and songs:
much less vocal than other jays; gives a variety of harsh chatters and clear whistles

On the move:
usually in small family groups flying through the forest

What they eat:
insects, seeds, fruit, and nuts; visits seed feeders

Nest:
cup; Dad and Mom build it together

Eggs, chicks, and childcare:
3–4 grayish-white eggs, some with fine marks; Mom **incubates** the eggs; both parents feed the young

Spends the winter:
in Washington

REAL QUICK

Size
$11^1/_2$"

Nest
CUP

Feeder
TUBE OR SUET

year-round

SAW IT!

STAN'S COOL STUFF

This jay is sometimes called "Camp Robber" because it comes to camps looking for food handouts. It is very tame and will fly to your hand if offered food. They store extra food for winter. Some people think they look like overgrown chickadees.

Clark's Nutcracker

Look for the white patches on the wings

What to look for:

a gray bird with black wings and a short tail; a narrow black band down the center of tail, a white undertail, and small white patches on the trailing edge of long wings are all best seen in flight

Where you'll find them:

at higher elevations in **coniferous** forests

Calls and songs:

no song but a wide variety of **calls**; most are raspy or metallic sounding

On the move:

long, direct flights across vast openings

What they eat:

seeds, insects, berries, eggs, and small mammals

Nest:

cup; Mom and Dad work together to build it

Eggs, chicks, and childcare:

2–5 pale-green eggs with brown marks; Mom and Dad sit on the eggs and feed the young

Spends the winter:

in Washington

REAL QUICK

Size
12"

Nest
CUP

Feeder
NONE

year-round

SAW IT!

STAN'S COOL STUFF

These birds have a pouch under the tongue to hold and transport up to 100 seeds. They rely heavily on pine seeds, storing large amounts to consume later. Some of these stored seeds are fed to the nestlings.

Rock Pigeon

Look for the gleaming, iridescent patches

What to look for:
color pattern varies; usually shades of gray with gleaming, **iridescent** patches of green mixed with blue; often has a light rump patch

Where you'll find them:
nearly anyplace where it can scratch for seeds

Calls and songs:
a series of coos, usually given during a **display**

On the move:
typically in small to large **flocks**; flaps rapidly, then glides with wings in a V shape

What they eat:
seeds and fruit; visits ground and seed feeders

Nest:
platform on a building, balcony, barn or shed, or under a bridge

Eggs, chicks, and childcare:
1–2 white eggs; Mom and Dad sit on the eggs and **regurgitate** a liquid, called **crop-milk**, to feed to the young (**squab**) for their first few days of life

Spends the winter:
in Washington

REAL QUICK

Size
13"

Nest
PLATFORM

Feeder
GROUND

year-round

SAW IT!

STAN'S COOL STUFF

The Rock Pigeon was introduced to North America by early settlers from Europe. Years of breeding in captivity have made it one of the few birds that has a variety of colors. It's also one of the few birds that can drink without tilting its head back.

Cooper's Hawk

Look for the banded, rounded tail

What to look for:
gray back, rusty chest, short wings, dark-red eyes, and a long tail with black bands and a rounded tip

Where you'll find them:
variety of **habitats,** from woodlands to backyards and parks

Calls and songs:
calls a loud, clear "cack-cack-cack-cack"

On the move:
flies with a few quick flaps followed by long glides

What they eat:
small birds (hunts birds at feeders) and mammals

Nest:
platform made with sticks and leaves, secured high in a tree; Dad and Mom build it together

Eggs, chicks, and childcare:
2–4 greenish eggs with brown marks; parents take turns sitting on the eggs and feeding the young

Spends the winter:
in Washington; moves around during winter to find food

REAL QUICK

Size
14–20"

Nest
PLATFORM

Feeder
NONE

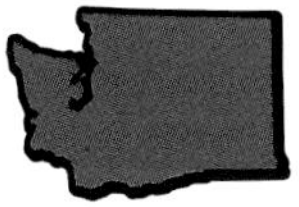

year-round

SAW IT!

STAN'S COOL STUFF

The stubby wings help this medium-sized hawk move around trees while it chases smaller birds. It will ambush **prey**, flying into brush and running after the birds that flee. **Fledglings** have gray eyes that turn yellow at 1 year and dark red after 3–5 years.

Peregrine Falcon

Look for the yellow eye-ring

What to look for:
dark-gray back; tan-to-white chest; dark **hood** head marking; wide black mustache; yellow eye-ring, base of bill, and legs; horizontal bars on belly, legs, and undertail; female is similar to male but noticeably larger

Where you'll find them:
canyons, open country, and cities with tall buildings

Calls and songs:
alarm **call** is a series of high-pitched screams

On the move:
fast direct flight with constant wingbeats

What they eat:
birds, such as Rock Pigeons in cities and shorebirds and **waterfowl** in rural areas

Nest:
ground (scrape) on a cliff edge, tall building, bridge, or smokestack

Eggs, chicks, and childcare:
3–4 white eggs with brown marks; parents take turns sitting on the eggs and feeding the young

Spends the winter:
some stay in Washington; others migrate

REAL QUICK

Size
16–20"

Nest
GROUND

Feeder
NONE

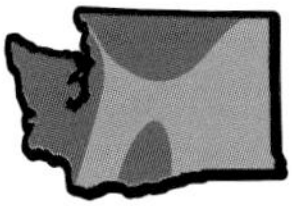

year-round
migration

SAW IT!

STAN'S COOL STUFF

Peregrine Falcons were once nearly eliminated due to shooting and trapping. Now they are doing well in most parts of the country. This is the fastest bird on the planet. It can fly 70 miles per hour in level flight and can dive up to 200 miles per hour.

Northern Harrier

Look for the large white rump patch

What to look for:
mostly gray with white belly and under wings

Where you'll find them:
open fields, swamps, cattail marshes, and prairies

Calls and songs:
usually silent; fast series of "kek" notes lasting 1–2 seconds

On the move:
low to ground, following contour of the land

What they eat:
small animals, snakes, and large bugs

Nest:
on ground, usually under dense shrub

Eggs, chicks, and childcare:
4–8 bluish-white eggs; Mom sits on the eggs; both parents provide for the youngsters

Spends the winter:
in Washington

REAL QUICK

Size
18–22"

Nest
GROUND

Feeder
NONE

year-round
summer

SAW IT!

STAN'S COOL STUFF

Also called Marsh Hawk, one of the few species of **raptor** where males and females don't look alike. It has facial disks like an owl, but it is a type of hawk. It uses its good sense of hearing to find prey when flying close to the ground

Canada Goose

Look for the white cheek strap

What to look for:
large gray goose with a black neck and head, and a white chin and cheek strap

Where you'll find them:
wetlands, ponds, lakes, rivers, and just about any **habitat** with some water

Calls and songs:
belts out its classic "honk-honk-honk," especially during flight

On the move:
flies in a **flock** in a large V shape when traveling long distances

What they eat:
aquatic plants, insects, and seeds

Nest:
ground nest of **vegetation** formed into a mound, usually very near or on water

Eggs, chicks, and childcare:
5–10 white eggs; Mom **incubates** the eggs; young follow the parents around and learn what to eat

Spends the winter:
in Washington; moves around to find open water in winter

REAL QUICK

Size
25–43"

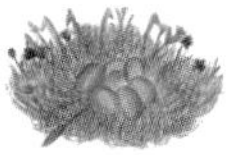

Nest
GROUND

Feeder
NONE

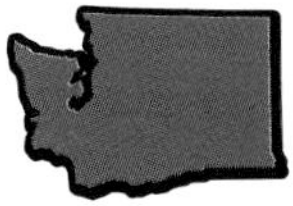

year-round

SAW IT!

STAN'S COOL STUFF

Males guard the flock, bobbing their heads and hissing whenever people approach. Adults **molt** their flight feathers while raising the young, making families temporarily flightless. Canada Geese start to breed in their third year. Adults stay together for many years.

Great Blue Heron

Look for the long yellow bill

What to look for:
tall gray heron with black eyebrows that end in plumes off the back of the head, neck feathers that drop down like a necklace, and a long yellow bill

Where you'll find them:
open water, from small ponds to large lakes

Calls and songs:
when startled, it barks repeatedly like a dog and keeps at it while flying away

On the move:
holds its neck in an S shape in flight and slightly cups its wings, trailing its legs straight out behind

What they eat:
small fish, frogs, insects, snakes, and baby birds

Nest:
platform; in a tree near or over open water; in a **colony** of up to 100 birds

Eggs, chicks, and childcare:
3–5 blue-green eggs; parents incubate the eggs and feed the **brood**

Spends the winter:
some stay in Washington; moves around to find open water

REAL QUICK

Size
42–48"

Nest
PLATFORM

Feeder
NONE

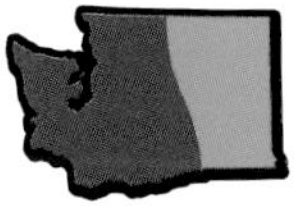

year-round
summer

SAW IT!

STAN'S COOL STUFF

The Great Blue is one of the most common herons in Washington. It stalks fish in shallow water and strikes at mice, squirrels, and anything else it can capture on land. Red-winged Blackbirds (pg. 25) often attack it to prevent it from taking the babies out of their nests.

Sandhill Crane

Look for the red cap

What to look for:
super-tall gray crane with a long neck and legs and a scarlet-red cap; wings and body are often stained rusty-brown

Where you'll find them:
wetlands, small and large

Calls and songs:
a very loud and distinctive rattling **call**, often heard before the bird is seen; call is one of the loudest due to a very long windpipe (**trachea**)

On the move:
wings look like they're flicking in flight, with the upstroke quicker than the downstroke; can fly at great heights of over 10,000 feet

What they eat:
insects, fruit, worms, plants, and amphibians

Nest:
ground nest of aquatic plants shaped into a mound

Eggs, chicks, and childcare:
2 olive-colored eggs with brown marks; Mom and Dad sit on the eggs; to get fed, babies follow their parents

Spends the winter:
in southwestern states and Mexico

REAL QUICK

Size
42-48"

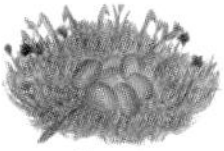

Nest
GROUND

Feeder
NONE

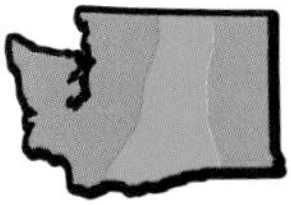

summer
migration

SAW ☑ IT!

STAN'S COOL STUFF

The Sandhill is one of the tallest birds in the country. Sandhills do a cool mating dance: a pair will first bow, then jump, cackle loudly, flap their wings, and finally, flip sticks and grass into the air.

Anna's Hummingbird

Look for the deep rose-red head

What to look for:
an **iridescent** green body with a dull gray breast and belly; a white eye-ring; and a dark head, chin, and neck that reflect rose-red in direct sunlight; female is similar to the male, but the dark area on the head reflects only a few red flecks

Where you'll find them:
both urban and suburban; **chaparral,** coastal scrub, and oak woodlands

Calls and songs:
a long series of buzzes and chips

On the move:
quick direct flight to prominent perches

What they eat:
nectar and insects; visits nectar feeders

Nest:
cup; Mom builds

Eggs, chicks, and childcare:
1–3 white eggs; Mom does all egg and chick care

Spends the winter:
on the coast of southern California and Mexico; some don't **migrate**

REAL QUICK

Size
4"

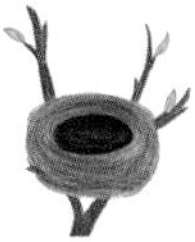

Nest
CUP

Feeder
NECTAR

year-round

SAW IT!

STAN'S COOL STUFF

This is a common hummer of backyards. The female builds a tiny nest low in a shrub or a small tree. Males put on a diving **display** to show off for females. At the bottom of their dive, wind rushing through their tail feathers makes a quick squeak.

Violet-green Swallow

Look for the emerald-green crown

What to look for:
dull emerald-green crown, **nape**, and back; violet-blue wings and tail; white chest, belly, and cheeks, with white extending above the eyes; wings extend beyond the tail when perching; female is similar but duller

Where you'll find them:
open **coniferous** and **deciduous** forests with dead trees

Calls and songs:
a series of high-pitched chips, usually before sunrise

On the move:
quick, darting flight

What they eat:
insects

Nest:
an old woodpecker cavity or a nest box; Mom and Dad build a small nest of stems and twigs inside

Eggs, chicks, and childcare:
4–6 white eggs with brown marks; Mom sits on the eggs; Mom and Dad feed the babies

Spends the winter:
in Mexico and Central America

REAL QUICK

Size
5¼"

Nest
CAVITY

Feeder
NONE

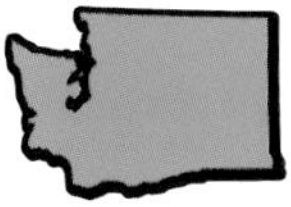

summer

SAW ✓ **IT!**

STAN'S COOL STUFF

Found throughout most of Washington in higher elevations. They can be attracted to nest boxes. They use feathers that they find to help line the nest. Violet-green Swallows can fly almost 30 miles per hour.

Wood Duck

Look for the boldly patterned head

pg. 113

What to look for:

boldly patterned head and crest with bold white outlines; rusty chest and white belly

Where you'll find them:

quiet, shallow ponds and deep in the woods, high up on tree branches

Calls and songs:

male **calls** a zipper-like "zeeeet"; female calls "oo-eek, oo-eek" loudly if startled and at takeoff

On the move:

blasts off from the water with loud calls and noisy wings; flies quickly through forest; enters cavity nest from full flight; small, tight group flights

What they eat:

aquatic insects, plants, and seeds

Nest:

cavity; adds a lining of soft, downy feathers in an old woodpecker hole or a nest box

Eggs, chicks, and childcare:

10–15 creamy-white eggs; only Mom **incubates** the eggs and shows the kids how to feed

Spends the winter:

in southwestern states; some stay in Washington

REAL QUICK

Size
17-20"

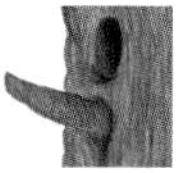

Nest
CAVITY

Feeder
NONE

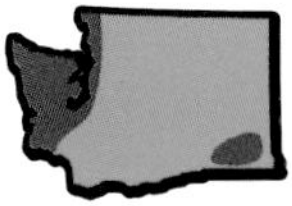

year-round
summer

SAW IT!

STAN'S COOL STUFF

This is a small dabbling duck. The female lays some eggs in a neighbor's nest (**egg dumping**), sometimes resulting in 20 or more eggs in a nest! The young stay in the nest for a day after hatching, then jump from as high as 60 feet to the ground or water to follow mom.

Mallard

Look for the green head

FEMALE
pg. 115

What to look for:
green head with a white **necklace**, rusty-brown chest, gray sides, yellow bill, orange legs and feet

Where you'll find them:
lakes and ponds, rivers and streams, and maybe even your backyard

Calls and songs:
the male doesn't quack; when you think of how a duck sounds, it's based on the female Mallard's classic loud quack

On the move:
sometimes in huge **flocks** with hundreds of ducks; mostly in small flocks of 6–10, especially in spring

What they eat:
seeds, aquatic plants, and insects; visits ground feeders offering corn

Nest:
ground nest; Mom builds it from plants nearby

Eggs, chicks, and childcare:
7–10 greenish-to-whitish eggs; Mom **incubates** the eggs and leads the young to food

Spends the winter:
in Washington

REAL QUICK

Size
19–21"

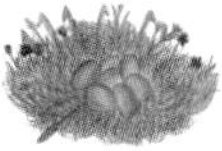

Nest
GROUND

Feeder
GROUND

year-round

SAW IT!

STAN'S COOL STUFF

This is a dabbling duck, tipping forward in shallow water to eat plants on the bottom. Only the male has black feathers in the center of its tail that curl upward. The name "Mallard" means "male" and refers to the males, which don't help raise their young.

Northern Shoveler

Look for the large, shovel-like bill

What to look for:
shiny, **iridescent** green head with rusty sides, a white chest, and a super-large, spoon-shaped bill

Where you'll find them:
shallow wetlands, ponds, and small lakes

Calls and songs:
male gives a crazy-sounding combination of popping and quacking, calling, "puk-puk, puk-puk, puk-puk"; female gives a classic quack **call**

On the move:
swims in tight circles, stirring up insects to eat; small **flocks** of 5–10 birds swim with bills pointing toward the water; flocks fly in tight formation

What they eat:
enjoys aquatic insects; likes plants, too

Nest:
ground nest; Mom forms plant material into a circle

Eggs, chicks, and childcare:
9–12 olive-colored eggs; Mom sits on the eggs and leads her little shovelers to food

Spends the winter:
in southwestern states, Mexico, and Central America; some stay in Washington

REAL QUICK

Size
19–21"

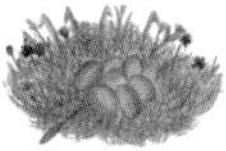

Nest
GROUND

Feeder
NONE

year-round
summer

SAW IT!

STAN'S COOL STUFF

The Northern Shoveler is a medium-sized duck. It is the only shoveler species found in North America. The name "Shoveler" refers to its peculiar, shovel-like bill. It feeds by using its bill to sift tiny aquatic insects and plants floating on the water's surface.

Common Merganser

Look for the long pointed orange bill

What to look for:
dark-green head with mostly white body; large orange bill

Where you'll find them:
lakes and large rivers

Calls and songs:
usually silent; female gives rapid croaking **call**

On the move:
super fast, low flying across surface of water; in groups in winter and pair in summer

What they eat:
small fish, aquatic insects, and amphibians

Nest:
cavity nest; Mom lines an old woodpecker hole or natural cavity

Eggs, chicks, and childcare:
9–11 ivory-colored eggs; Mom sits on the eggs and feeds the young

Spends the winter:
in Washington; moves around to find open water

REAL QUICK

Size
26–28"

Nest
CAVITY

Feeder
NONE

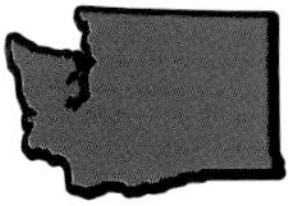

year-round

SAW IT!

STAN'S COOL STUFF

One of the fastest-flying birds in level flight. Doesn't have teeth but has a wicked-cool saw-like edge on its bill to hold onto slippery fish. This is why they are sometimes called Saw-bills. Babies leave the nest and find their own food 24 hours after hatching.

Rufous Hummingbird

Look for the orange-red throat patch

MALE

FEMALE

What to look for:

tiny orange bird with a white chest and green-to-tan flanks; male has a black throat patch (gorget) that reflects orange-red in sunlight; female lacks the throat patch

Where you'll find them:

all across the western half of the state during **migration**

Calls and songs:

fast series of chip notes

On the move:

very fast flyers, but hovers around flowers and **nectar** feeders

What they eat:

nectar and insects; visits nectar feeders

Nest:

cup; Mom builds it

Eggs, chicks, and childcare:

1–3 white eggs; Mom sits on the eggs and feeds the babies

Spends the winter:

in Central and South America; some stay all winter

REAL QUICK

Size
$3^3/_4$"

Nest
CUP

Feeder
NECTAR

year-round

SAW IT!

STAN'S COOL STUFF

One of the smallest birds in the state, they weigh only 2–3 grams. A very durable bird with some staying all winter even though food is scarce. They are very bold and protective of their nests and food, chasing away larger birds and other hummingbirds.

Bullock's Oriole

Look for the black eye line

pg. 213

What to look for:
a bright orange-and-black bird with a black crown, eye line, **nape,** chin, back, and wings, and a bold white patch on the wings

Where you'll find them:
cottonwood groves, open forests

Calls and songs:
a rich musical song

On the move:
slow direct flight from tree to tree

What they eat:
insects, berries, and **nectar;** comes to nectar, orange-half, and grape jelly feeders

Nest:
pendulous; Mom and Dad build it

Eggs, chicks, and childcare:
4–6 pale white-to-gray eggs with brown marks; Mom sits on the eggs; Mom and Dad feed the children

Spends the winter:
in Central and South America

REAL QUICK

Size
8"

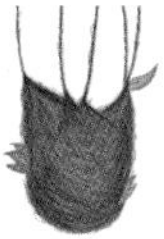

Nest
PENDULOUS

Feeder
NECTAR

summer

SAW IT!

STAN'S COOL STUFF

Bullock's and Baltimore Orioles are closely related and were once considered the same species. They use long plant fibers to create a sock-like nest. One of the few species that will eject cowbird eggs from their nests. Often comes to nectar feeders for a sweet treat.

Black-headed Grosbeak

Look for the black head, tail and wings

What to look for:

a stocky bird with a burnt-orange chest, neck, and rump; a black head, tail, and wings; a large bill with the upper bill darker than the lower; and irregularly shaped white wing patches

Where you'll find them:

wide variety of **habitats,** mostly in foothills and lower elevations

Calls and songs:

both males and females sing a rich song, similar to American Robins

On the move:

quick, fast flight

What they eat:

seeds, insects, and fruit; visits seed feeders

Nest:

cup; Mom builds it

Eggs, chicks, and childcare:

3–4 pale-green or bluish eggs with brown marks; Mom and Dad sit on the eggs and feed the kids

Spends the winter:

in Mexico, Central America, and South America

REAL QUICK

Size
8"

Nest
CUP

Feeder
HOPPER

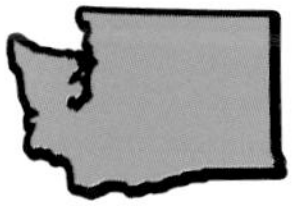

summer

SAW IT!

STAN'S COOL STUFF

Both the male and female sing and defend their territory. The large bill is used to crush seeds and also hard-bodied insects, such as beetles and spiders. Monarch butterflies are poisonous to most birds, but Black-headed Grosbeaks can eat them without getting sick.

Varied Thrush

Look for the orange eyebrows

What to look for:
male is a potbellied robin-like bird with orange eyebrows, chin, breast, and wing bars; a gray-to-blue head, neck, and back; and a black breast band and eye mark; female is a browner version of the male and lacks the black breast band

Where you'll find them:
coniferous forests; seen foraging on the ground

Calls and songs:
a blurry flute-like single note

On the move:
strong flight from ground to tree

What they eat:
bugs and fruit

Nest:
cup; Mom builds it

Eggs, chicks, and childcare:
3–5 pale-blue eggs with brown marks; Mom and Dad sit on the eggs and give food to the babies

Spends the winter:
in West Coast states; some don't **migrate**

REAL QUICK

Size
9½"

Nest
CUP

Feeder
GROUND

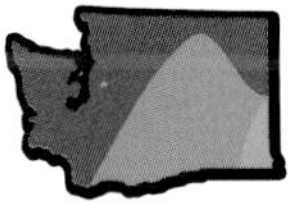

year-round
summer
winter

SAW IT!

STAN'S COOL STUFF

This thrush is a very colorful bird, usually seen on the ground, feeding on insects. They are often seen in small **flocks** during winter. Their population declined more than 70% from 1966 to 2015.

House Finch

Look for the reddish face and the brown cap

MALE

YELLOW MALE

FEMALE
pg. 69

What to look for:
red-to-orange face, throat, chest, and rump, and a brown cap

Where you'll find them:
forests, city and suburban areas, around homes, parks, and farms

Calls and songs:
male sings a loud, cheerful **warbling** song

On the move:
moves around in small family units; never travels long distances

What they eat:
seeds, fruit, and leaf buds; comes to seed feeders and feeders with a glop of grape jelly

Nest:
cup, but occasionally in a cavity; likes to nest in a hanging flower basket or on a front door wreath

Eggs, chicks, and childcare:
4–5 pale-blue eggs, lightly marked; Mom sits on the eggs and Dad feeds her while she **incubates**; Mom and Dad feed the **brood**

Spends the winter:
in Washington; moves around to find food

REAL QUICK

Size
5"

Nest
CUP

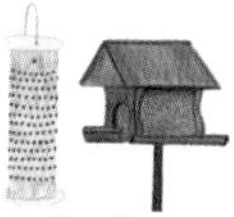

Feeder
TUBE OR HOPPER

year-round

SAW IT!

STAN'S COOL STUFF

The House Finch is very social and is found across the country. It can be a common bird at feeders. Unfortunately, it suffers from a fatal eye disease that causes the eyes to crust over. It's rare to see a yellow male; yellow **plumage** may be a result of a poor diet.

Purple Finch

Look for the raspberry red head

MALE

FEMALE

pg. 79

What to look for:
raspberry-red head, **nape**, back, and wings; dark patch behind eye

Where you'll find them:
suburban areas, around homes, parks, and forests

Calls and songs:
male sings a clear cheerful song

On the move:
in **flocks** in winter; pairs in nesting season

What they eat:
seeds, fruit, and insects; comes to seed feeders

Nest:
cup; often on far end of **conifer** branch or close to trunk in **deciduous** trees

Eggs, chicks, and childcare:
4–5 greenish-blue eggs with brown markings; Mom sits on the eggs; Mom and Dad feed the **brood**

Spends the winter:
in Washington; moves around to find food

REAL QUICK

Size
6"

Nest
CUP

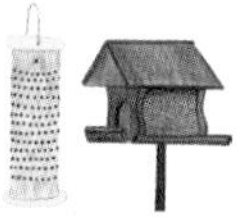

Feeder
TUBE OR HOPPER

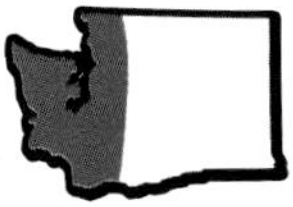

year-round

SAW IT!

STAN'S COOL STUFF

A highly **migratory** bird that moves around a lot in winter. Often comes to feeders in groups of males and females. Large bill helps crack open seeds to extract the nut.

Common Merganser

Look for the rust-red ragged "hair"

What to look for:
rust-red head and ragged "hair;" gray body and white chest and chin; long, pointed, orange bill

Where you'll find them:
lakes and large rivers

Calls and songs:
usually silent; female gives rapid croaking **call**

On the move:
super fast, low flying across surface of water; in groups in winter and pair in summer

What they eat:
small fish, aquatic insects, and amphibians

Nest:
cavity nest; Mom lines an old woodpecker hole or natural cavity

Eggs, chicks, and childcare:
9–11 ivory-colored eggs; Mom sits on the eggs and feeds the young

Spends the winter:
in Washington; moves around to find open water

REAL QUICK

Size
26–28"

Nest
CAVITY

Feeder
NONE

year-round

SAW IT!

STAN'S COOL STUFF

One of the fastest-flying birds in level flight. Doesn't have teeth but has a wicked-cool saw-like edge on its bill to hold onto slippery fish. This is why they are sometimes called Saw-bills. Babies leave the nest and find their own food 24 hours after hatching.

Ring-billed Gull

Look for the black ring on the bill

What to look for:
white gull with gray wings and a yellow bill with a black ring near the tip; winter **plumage** has speckles on the head and neck

Where you'll find them:
shores of large lakes and rivers; often at garbage dumps and parking lots

Calls and songs:
calls out a wide variety of loud, rising squawks and squeals—classic gull sounds

On the move:
strong flight with constant wing flaps

What they eat:
insects and fish; it also picks through garbage, scavenging for other food

Nest:
ground nest; defends a small area around it

Eggs, chicks, and childcare:
2–4 off-white eggs with brown marks; Mom and Dad take turns **incubating** the eggs and feeding their young

Spends the winter:
in Washington

REAL QUICK

Size
18–20"

Nest
GROUND

Feeder
NONE

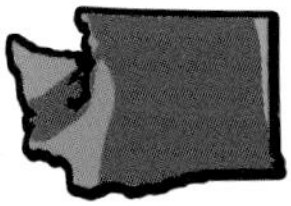

year-round
summer
winter

SAW IT!

STAN'S COOL STUFF

This is one of the most common gulls in the country. Hundreds of these birds often **flock** together. The ring on the bill appears after the first winter. In the fall of the first three years, the birds have a different plumage. In the third year, they grow adult plumage.

California Gull

Look for the red-and-black mark on lower bill

What to look for:
a white bird with gray wings, black wing tips, a red-and-black mark on the tip of a yellow bill, and a red ring around dark eyes; winter adult has brown streaks on the back of the head and **nape** of neck

Where to find them:
coastal areas

Calls and songs:
classic gull-type **call,** hoarse series of "uh-uh-uh"

On the move:
standing on the ground or gliding in the air on outstretched wings

What they eat:
insects, seeds, and mammals

Nest:
ground nest; Mom and Dad built it and line it with grass and seaweed; nests in a **colony**

Eggs, chicks, and childcare:
2–5 pale-brown or olive-colored eggs; Mom and Dad take turns sitting on the eggs and feeding the babies

Spends the winter:
along western coastal US and Mexico; some don't **migrate**

REAL QUICK

Size
20–22"

Nest
GROUND

Feeder
NONE

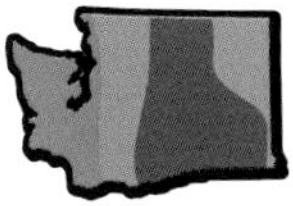

year-round
migration
winter

SAW IT!

STAN'S COOL STUFF

California Gulls travel up to 40 miles to find food. They will eat just about anything they find. Usually they are seen in small groups. Their population is stable to slightly declining over past 50 years.

Herring Gull

Look for the orange-red mark on lower bill

What to look for:
mostly white with gray back and wings; yellow bill with reddish-orange spot on lower bill

Where to find them:
usually not far away from water

Calls and songs:
classic gull **call**; more variety than other gull species

On the move:
strong high flyers; moves around in groups

What they eat:
fish, insects, clams, eggs, and baby birds

Nest:
on ground on islands or near water

Eggs, chicks, and childcare:
2–3 olive-colored eggs with brown marks; Mom and Dad take turns sitting on the eggs and feeding the babies

Spends the winter:
in Washington

REAL QUICK

Size
23–26"

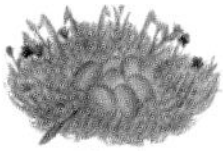

Nest
GROUND

Feeder
NONE

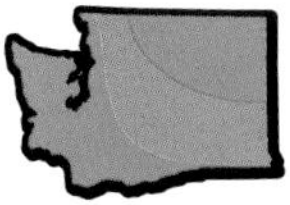

migration
winter

SAW IT!

STAN'S COOL STUFF

Often seen following fishing boats looking for a handout. Most common along the Pacific Coast but often seen well inland away from the ocean. Usually drinks fresh water but can also drink sea water, excreting excess salt out of glands at base of bill.

Snow Goose

Look for the pink bill

What to look for:
white **morph** has black wing tips and patches of black and brown; blue morph has a white head and a gray breast and back; both morphs have a pink bill and legs

Where you'll find them:
wide-open fields, wetlands, and lakes of any size

Calls and songs:
one of the noisiest of all **waterfowl**; both male and female give high-pitched, nasally "honk"

On the move:
in large **flocks**

What they eat:
aquatic insects and green plants

Nest:
ground; Mom builds it

Eggs, chicks, and childcare:
3–5 white eggs; Mom **incubates** the eggs; Mom and Dad teach the young to feed

Spends the winter:
in parts of Washington, Oregon, California, and Arizona

REAL QUICK

Size
25–38"

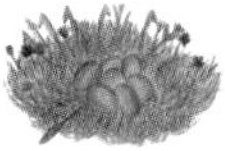

Nest
GROUND

Feeder
NONE

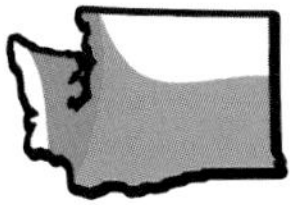

migration
winter

SAW IT!

STAN'S COOL STUFF

Snow Geese nest in the Arctic and **migrate** all the way to Washington, Oregon, and down to southern border states, and Mexico. A group of Snow Geese is called a "gaggle." They are almost always seen in large flocks, which helps them stay safe from predators.

American Goldfinch

Look for the black forehead

What to look for:

male is a bright canary-yellow bird with a black forehead, wings, and tail; female is olive-yellow and lacks a black forehead; winter male resembles the female

Where you'll find them:

open fields, scrubby areas, woodlands, backyards

Calls and songs:

male sings a pleasant high-pitched song; gives **twitter calls** during flight

On the move:

appears roller coaster-like in flight

What they eat:

loves seeds and insects; comes to seed (especially thistle) feeders

Nest:

cup; lines the cup with the soft, silky down from wild thistle

Eggs, chicks, and childcare:

4–6 pale-blue eggs; Mom **incubates** the eggs and Dad pitches in to help her feed the babies

Spends the winter:

in Washington; **flocks** of up to 20 birds move around in winter

REAL QUICK

Size
5"

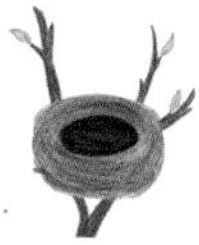

Nest
CUP

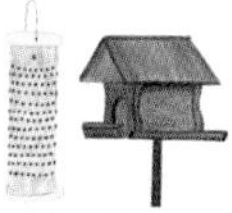

Feeder
TUBE OR HOPPER

year-round

SAW IT!

STAN'S COOL STUFF

The American Goldfinch is often called Wild Canary due to its canary-colored **plumage**. This cute little feeder bird is almost always in small **flocks**, visiting thistle tube feeders that offer Nyjer seed. A late-nesting bird with most nesting in August.

Yellow Warbler

Look for the orange streaks on the chest

What to look for:

yellow bird with thin orange streaks on the chest and belly; female lacks orange streaks

Where you'll find them:

gardens and shrubby areas near water, backyards

Calls and songs:

male sings a string of sweet notes, sounding like "sweet, sweet, sweet, I'm-so-sweet!"

On the move:

zooms around shrubs and shorter trees; begins to **migrate** south in August, migrating at night in mixed **flocks** of warblers; males return to claim territories 1–2 weeks before females arrive

What they eat:

insects

Nest:

cup; Mom builds it

Eggs, chicks, and childcare:

4–5 white eggs with brown marks; Mom sits on the eggs; Mom and Dad give food to the kids

Spends the winter:

in California, Mexico, Central America, and South America

REAL QUICK

Size
5"

Nest
CUP

Feeder
NONE

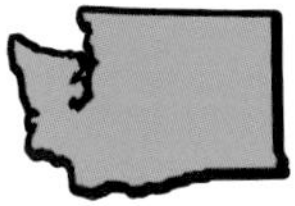

summer

SAW IT!

STAN'S COOL STUFF

The Yellow Warbler is common and widespread in Washington. It eats small caterpillars and many other bugs on tree leaves. The male is easier to see higher up in trees than the duller female. He sings loudly, zips off to grab a bug, and then starts singing again.

Bullock's Oriole

Look for the dull yellow head and chest

FEMALE

MALE
pg. 189

What to look for:

dull-yellow head and chest, gray-to-black wings with white wing bars, a pale white belly, and a gray back, seen in flight

Where you'll find them:

cottonwood groves and open forests

Calls and songs:

a rich musical song

On the move:

slow direct flight from tree to tree

What they eat:

insects, berries, and **nectar;** comes to nectar, orange-half, and grape jelly feeders

Nest:

pendulous; Mom and Dad build it

Eggs, chicks, and childcare:

4–6 pale white-to-gray eggs with brown marks; Mom sits on the eggs; Mom and Dad feed the children

Spends the winter:

in Central and South America

REAL QUICK

Size
8"

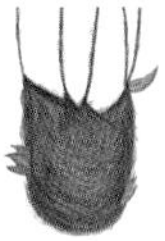

Nest
PENDULOUS

Feeder
NECTAR

summer

SAW IT!

STAN'S COOL STUFF

Bullock's and Baltimore Orioles are closely related and were once considered the same species. They use long plant fibers to create a sock-like nest. One of the few species that will eject cowbird eggs from their nests. Often comes to nectar feeders for a sweet treat.

Western Tanager

Look for the red head

What to look for:

male is a bright yellow bird with a red head; black back, tail, and wings; and one white and one yellow wing bar; non-breeding male lacks the red head; the female is duller than the male, lacking the red head

Where you'll find them:

most common in **coniferous** forests

Calls and songs:

a rich raspy song lasting 2–3 seconds, repeated

On the move:

fast, direct flight from tree top to tree top

What they eat:

insects and fruit

Nest:

cup; Mom builds it

Eggs, chicks, and childcare:

3–5 light-blue eggs with brown marks; Mom sits on the eggs; Mom and Dad give food to the kids

Spends the winter:

in Mexico and Central America

REAL QUICK

Size
7¼"

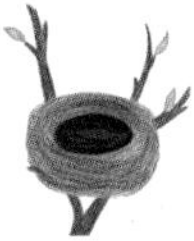

Nest
CUP

Feeder
NONE

summer
migration

SAW IT!

STAN'S COOL STUFF

A beautiful bird usually nesting in coniferous trees in Washington. The male will feed the female while she is **incubating** eggs. During breeding season, they mainly eat insects, but they will also eat fruit later in the year.

Western Kingbird

Look for the bright-yellow belly

What to look for:
bright-yellow belly and yellow underwings; gray head and chest, often with white chin; wings and tail are dark gray to nearly black with white outer edges on the tail

Where you'll find them:
open country, shrubby areas, farms, homesteads

Calls and songs:
a series of sharp "kips"

On the move:
flies to prominent perches with quick, continuous wingbeats

What they eat:
insects and berries

Nest:
cup; Mom and Dad build it

Eggs, chicks, and childcare:
3–4 white eggs with brown marks; Mom **incubates** the eggs; Mom and Dad feed the babies

Spends the winter:
in Mexico and Central America

REAL QUICK

Size
9"

Nest
CUP

Feeder
NONE

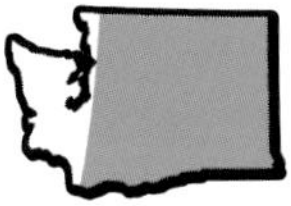

summer

SAW IT!

STAN'S COOL STUFF

Western Kingbirds spend a lot of time perched on fence posts and small trees, watching for insects to eat, such as crickets and grasshoppers. Adults teach the young to hunt by bringing injured insects back for them to chase.

Western Meadowlark

Look for the V-shaped black necklace

What to look for:

a robin-shaped bird with a yellow chest and belly, a V-shaped black **necklace,** a short tail, and white outer tail feathers that are usually seen when flying away

Where to find them:

meadows, open grassy country, and roadsides

Calls and songs:

sings a wonderfully clear flute-like whistling song

On the move:

if you move toward it when it's perching on a fence post, it will quickly dive into tall grass

What they eat:

insects and seeds

Nest:

cup; on the ground in dense **cover**; Mom builds the nest by herself

Eggs, chicks, and childcare:

3–5 white eggs with brown marks; Mom sits on the eggs, but both parents feed the **hatchlings**

Spends the winter:

in western Washington; moves around to find food

REAL QUICK

Size
9"

Nest
CUP

Feeder
NONE

year-round
summer

SAW IT!

STAN'S COOL STUFF

They are members of the blackbird family, which makes them relatives of orioles and grackles. Like most ground-dwelling birds, their populations have gone down greatly in the last 50 years. A wonderful songster, this bird often runs around before flying.

BIRD FOOD FUN FOR THE FAMILY

If you and your family like to do fun projects together, making your own bird food and bird-feeding items might be just the right ones to try. Chances are good that you already have most of the ingredients at home to make delicious and nutritious treats for your wild bird friends.

You'll be doing these projects in the kitchen, so show your mom or dad the following sections. They're written specifically with the whole family in mind. For example, you may need to check with a parent or guardian for help with such tasks as grocery shopping, stovetop cooking, or food preparation, like cutting up fresh fruit.

Starter Snacks and Fruit Treats

You can start by offering some food that's already in your kitchen. Peanut butter attracts a lot of birds! Simply use a spatula to smear some on the bark of a nearby tree where you can watch it from a window. Or use a piece of firewood: prop it up or hang it with a rope and slather it with peanut butter—then watch the birds go wild.

To offer treats like raisins, dates, and currants, place them outside in a nonbreakable small bowl with a few holes drilled in the bottom for drainage. Waxwings, robins, and many other birds love small dried fruit, and some will be flying in shortly to get some.

Putting out fresh fruit, such as apples and oranges, is another great way to attract bright and colorful birds to your yard. Cut these into small, manageable pieces, and offer the snacks on the tray of a feeder.

Another cool way to serve an orange is to cut one in half and place the halves sunny-side up on a feeder or branch. This arrangement allows birds to easily feast on the sweet fruit contained inside the rind. Sometimes it's best to impale the orange half on a nail to stop it from rolling away.

Plain and unsalted nuts, especially peanuts, pecans, and walnuts, make wonderful treats for birds. Simply add these to a feeder tray with seeds or place them in a tube feeder for nuts.

Easy Bird Food Recipes

Preparing bird food of any kind shows that you care about the birds in your backyard. Now, are you ready to try making some recipes? Below are just a few suggestions. You can find much more online.

Sweet Homemade Nectar

Nectar is a superb food for many birds. Studies of nectar from flowers have shown that the average flower nectar is 25% sucrose. Sucrose is a simple sugar, so to make the correct strength of homemade nectar (sugar water), mix a ratio of 1 part sugar to 4 parts water. You'll discover that hummingbirds, orioles, and woodpeckers will thoroughly enjoy the sweet drink that you made.

INGREDIENTS
¼ cup granulated white sugar
1 cup warm water

DIRECTIONS: Add the sugar to the water and stir to dissolve. If you prefer, you can boil the water first so the sugar dissolves more quickly. Cool to room temperature before filling your feeder. Store any extra in the refrigerator or freezer.

NOTES: Never substitute brown sugar or honey for white sugar. Also, there is no need to add red food coloring because the birds will be attracted to any amount of red on any part of your **nectar** feeder.

Birds-Go-Wild Spread

INGREDIENTS
½ cup raisins
½ cup granola
½ cup oatmeal
½ cup Cheerios
16-ounce jar smooth peanut butter

DIRECTIONS: Mix dry ingredients in a large mixing bowl. Warm the peanut butter in a microwave or place the jar in warm water to soften. Scoop out the softened peanut butter and mix well with dry ingredients until smooth.

Spread on tree bark or smear a few dollops on the tray of a feeder.

Love-It-Nutty Butter

INGREDIENTS
2 cups shelled peanuts, unsalted
2 cups shelled walnuts, unsalted
¼ cup raisins
3–5 tablespoons coconut oil or other vegetable oil

DIRECTIONS: Toss dry ingredients into a food processor. Start blending. Add oil until the mixture reaches a smooth, thick consistency. Store in refrigerator.

Smear on a wooden board with grooves or spread on tree bark.

Make Your Own Suet

You and your family can make outstanding **suet** recipes at home, too. Suet is animal fat, often from cows, and there are several convenient ways to get it for your recipes.

A quick way is to purchase plain suet cakes. In store-bought suet, the fat has already been melted down (**rendered**). A cheaper way might be to buy fat trimmings in bulk from your local butcher or large amounts of **lard** at your grocery store. A clever way to get rendered fat from your own kitchen is for an adult to pour fat drippings from cooked bacon, pork, or beef into an empty, clean can. When the fat has cooled and solidified, cover and refrigerate to save for future use.

Easy-Peasy Suet

INGREDIENTS
1 cup solidified fat of your choice
1 cup chunky peanut butter
3 cups ground cornmeal
1 cup white flour
1 cup black oil sunflower seeds or peanuts

DIRECTIONS: In a large pot, melt the fat over low heat. Do not heat quickly or the fat might burn. Strain the fat through a **cheesecloth** to remove any chunks, and then pour the liquid back into the pot.

Add the peanut butter to the fat. Stir over low heat until the mixture melts and consistency is smooth. Remove from heat. Add the cornmeal and flour, and mix until stiff. Add the sunflower seeds or peanuts, and mix thoroughly.

Pour into a mold or container. With a spatula, spread out the mixture and smooth the top. Cool completely, then cut into squares. Store in freezer.

Simply Super Suet

INGREDIENTS
2 cups **suet** or **lard**
1 cup peanut butter
2 cups yellow cornmeal
2 cups cracked corn
1 cup black oil sunflower seeds

DIRECTIONS: In a large pot, melt the suet or lard over low heat. Add the peanut butter, stirring until melted and well mixed. Add remaining ingredients, and mix.

Pour into baking pans or forms and allow to cool. Cut into chunks or shapes. Store in freezer.

Yummy Bird-Feeding Projects

Bird-feeding projects are super activities for families, and they can be a big hit at special occasions, such as birthday parties. These very attractive ornaments and feeders also make unique gifts for the holidays and family celebrations.

Birdseed Ornaments

INGREDIENTS
cookie cutters in any shape
nonstick cooking spray
½ cup water
3 tablespoons white corn syrup
2½ teaspoons unflavored gelatin
¾ cup white flour
4 cups black oil sunflower seeds
10- to 12-inch pieces of string or **jute** twine

DIRECTIONS: Place the cookie cutters on wax paper and spray with nonstick cooking spray. Set aside.

In a saucepan, bring the water and corn syrup to a boil. Reduce heat and stir in gelatin until completely mixed. Do not overcook.

Transfer the hot liquid to a bowl. Add the flour, and mix until smooth. Add the sunflower seeds, and mix well. Mixture will now be thick.

Use a spatula to fill each cookie cutter. Be sure to press the seeds into all parts of the shapes. Roll any extra mixture into balls. Poke one hole through each shape and each ball with a pencil or similar object.

When cooled, pop out the ornaments from the cookie cutters. Thread a length of string or twine through each hole, and tie the ends to form a loop. Loop each of your ornaments over nearby branches, and watch the birds come to feast!

Pine Cone Birdseed Feeders

Try your hand at making this fabulous little bird feeder from an ordinary pine cone. It's fun and easy, and everyone in your family can make their own.

INGREDIENTS (per person)
1 pine cone
10- to 12-inch piece of string or **jute** twine
peanut butter
birdseed

DIRECTIONS: Tie a piece of string or twine to a pine cone. Roll the cone in peanut butter, filling the spaces between the "petals" (bracts) and coating the entire surface. Then roll the cone in birdseed until the seeds completely cover the peanut butter.

Hang the feeder outside where you can see the birds feeding on it, and enjoy the show!

MORE ACTIVITIES FOR THE BIRD-MINDED

Nothing brings family and friends closer together than a shared interest. Birding and backyard bird feeding are enjoyable, year-round activities that many find appealing. Here are some things to do that are not only fun for everyone but also supportive for the birds.

Help Birds Build Their Nests

A thoughtful way for the entire family to work together with birds during spring is to put out a variety of soft and flexible natural items to help birds build their nests.

First, gather some everyday materials around your home that birds will use. Here are some excellent items to offer:

- Yarn, cut into 6-inch-long pieces
- Fabric from an old, clean T-shirt, cut into 6-inch-long strips
- **Cotton batting** (used for handicrafts)
- Fuzzy pet hair from a brush

Next, place your materials into an unused, clean suet cage. Be sure to let the ends of the yarn and fabric strips hang out, and don't pack the material in tightly. The birds need to be able to take out the items easily.

Hang the cage by a short chain from a tree in early spring, when the birds are starting to construct their nests. And then, wait...

Soon, birds will be flying back and forth to the materials and choosing their favorites. It's a delight to see birds making use of your nesting contributions. Not only have you assisted the bird parents, but you've also helped them provide a comfy home for their families. Good job!

Make a Bird-Watching List

Making a watch list on **poster board** of the birds that have visited your yard is a handicraft project that the whole family will enjoy. You can decorate the poster any way you like, but it's awesome to show pictures of the birds you've spotted and write notes about the sightings.

Each time you see a new species in your yard, mark it on the poster with the date and time of day. Attach it to the refrigerator, or put it in another prominent place where it's easy for everyone in the family to see and add their updates.

Your watch list is also a valuable way to track the arrival of the first hummingbirds and orioles in your area each spring. If you create a new watch list each year, it could reveal trends in the arrival dates. This information would be of interest not only to your family and friends, but also to your teachers and local birding organizations.

Save the Birds with Hawk Cutouts

Another fun and important project is to make hawk cutouts to attach to your windows. These items will help prevent birds from flying into sheets of glass at your home.

In-flight window strikes are one of the major killers of our wild bird friends. Window reflections of the sky, trees, and other natural features in your yard create the illusion to birds that the flight path is clear. When birds see forms of predator birds in the reflections, they will turn away and take another route.

Various web pages show outlines (**silhouettes**) of hawks that you can print and cut out. Check the possibilities, and then pick your favorites.

Tape the cutouts to any large picture windows, as well as other windows and doors with clear glass. This preventive action will greatly reduce the risk of birds crashing headfirst into glass. Then give yourself a high five for helping to save them.

Build Your Very Own Birdhouse

A first-rate project for kids and adults to do together is to construct a birdhouse. Building plans are available online for different kinds of birdhouses for different kinds of birds. Give them a once-over, and pick one that you like best for the birds you want nesting nearby.

The instructions online will help you select the right kind of wood and show you how to cut it to the right sizes. Most importantly, the plans will provide the correct size of the entrance hole for the bird, along with how-to instructions for making it. Most birdhouse projects require hand and power tools, so be sure to work with an adult.

You might even want to make multiple birdhouses with your extended family or your neighbors. With everyone doing different tasks, your team can turn out a bluebird box, a wren box, a robin platform, and more!

Create a Bird-Friendly Yard

There is no better way to support the birds in your area than to plant bird-friendly flowers, bushes, and trees. There are many varieties of these plants, making it easy to choose some that will be ideal for your yard.

Planting perennials that bloom large and showy flowers each year is an outstanding way to feed hummingbirds. Many shrubs

produce attractive **nectar**-filled flowers and then, later in the summer, edible fruit, which the birds love. Numerous tree species offer berries and nuts—foods the birds depend on in late fall.

A yard with grass alone just isn't a friendly **habitat** for birds, so sit down with your family and think about putting in a flower garden or adorning your yard with some shrubs and trees. Soon afterward, you'll be hearing the sweet chirping of birds and a rich repertoire of **birdsong** all around you.

Take a Birding Trip

Everyone loves a good time! For a fun family outing, plan a birding trip to a local park, state park, or national wildlife refuge. In spring, you'll be rewarded with migrating warblers. During summer, all of the nesting birds will be feeding babies. In fall, **waterfowl** will be super active. Even in winter, there are many amazing birds to see.

Your local nature center is another good place to see birds. Oftentimes nature centers have bird feeders set up to attract birds. Stop in after school or early on Saturday mornings to see what comes to the feeders.

The shores along the Pacific Ocean are fantastic places where other incredible birds gather. Pack a picnic lunch and head out with your family to enjoy both the outdoors and the birds that don't hang around feeders. Cormorants and gulls are just some of the cool birds that spend their time around the water.

Practice Good Birding

Finding a stray feather or an empty bird nest is exciting when you and your family are sharing time in nature. Examining these wonders and making a sketch or taking photos are always fun educational opportunities. However, everyone should be aware that collecting, possessing, or owning wild bird feathers, nests, and even bird eggs is not permitted under federal law.

It may seem silly that a lost feather or vacant bird nest needs protecting, but very important laws stop people from buying, selling, and trading these items. In the past, a lively market for feathers, bird nests, and also eggs led to widespread killing of birds, some to near extinction. To prevent from this happening again, strong laws were passed to safeguard all of our bird species.

So enjoy seeing, studying, and learning about birds, but please don't take any feathers, nests, or eggs with you out of their natural environment. Leave them just as you found them, and perhaps someone else will also get the opportunity to benefit from studying them.

CITIZEN SCIENCE PROJECTS

I can't think of a more exciting way to learn about birds and expand the birding experience than to take part in a citizen science project. If you are unfamiliar with citizen science projects, they are sponsored by organizations in which citizens like yourself can contribute in a meaningful way to actual scientific projects right from your own home! Most projects don't take much time and can be fun family activities, with everyone sharing what they learned about birds.

There are simple citizen science projects that might have you just count the birds that come to your feeders. Others are more complex and involve more time, effort, and perhaps a little traveling. Either way, I'm sure you can find an enjoyable and educational citizen project that will be a perfect fit for your family. Give it a try!

Here are some popular projects and resources for you to explore:

The very well-known Christmas Bird Count winter census, FeederWatch, and more

birds.cornell.edu

Hummingbird migration

journeynorth.org/hummingbirds

Finding and counting nesting birds

nestwatch.org

General citizen science projects for counting birds

birdwatchingdaily.com/featured-stories/year-round-citizen-science-projects

American Kestrel nesting and population study

kestrel.peregrinefund.org

LEARNING ABOUT BIRDING ON THE INTERNET

Birding online is another fine way to discover more information about birds—plus it's a terrific way to spend time during rainy summer days and winter evenings after sunset. So check out the websites below, and be sure to share with your family and friends the fabulous things you've learned about birds.

eBird

ebird.org/home

American Birding Association: Young Birders

aba.org/aba-young-birders

Cornell Lab of Ornithology

birds.cornell.edu

Author Stan Tekiela's website

naturesmart.com

In addition, online birding groups can be of valuable assistance to you as well. Facebook has many pages dedicated to specific areas of the state and the birds that live there. These sites are an excellent, real-time resource that will help you spot birds in your region. Consider joining a Facebook birding group.

GLOSSARY

birdsong: A series of musical notes that a bird strings together in a pleasing melody. Also called a song.

brood: A family of bird brothers and sisters that hatched at around the same time.

brood parasites: Birds that don't nest, incubate, or raise families, such as Brown-headed Cowbirds (pg. 19 and 89). See *host*.

call: A nonmusical sound, often a single note, that is repeated.

carrion: A dead and often rotting animal's body, or carcass, that is an important food for many other animals, including birds.

chaparral: An area of scrubland and brush in the foothills and up mountain slopes. The trees and shrubs that grow there are adapted to the dry summers.

cheesecloth: A loosely woven cotton cloth that is used primarily to wrap cheese. It is also used to strain particles from liquids.

colony: A group of birds nesting together in the same area. The size of a colony can range from two pairs to hundreds of birds.

coniferous: A tree or shrub that has evergreen, needle-like leaves and that produces cones.

cotton batting: A light, soft cotton material, often used to stuff quilts.

cover: A dense area of trees or shrubs where birds nest or hide.

crop-milk: A liquid that pigeons and doves regurgitate (spit up) to feed their young.

crustaceans: A large, mainly aquatic group of critters, such as crayfish, crabs, and shrimp.

deciduous: A tree or shrub that sheds its leaves every year.

display: An attention-getting behavior of birds to impress and attract a mate, or to draw predators away from the nest. A display may include dramatic movements in flight or on the ground.

double-scratch: A quick double hop that some birds use to find food.

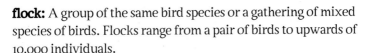

epaulets: Decorative color patches on the shoulders of a bird, as seen in male Red-winged Blackbirds (pg. 25).

excavate: To dig or carefully remove wood or dirt, creating a cavity, hole, or tunnel.

flock: A group of the same bird species or a gathering of mixed species of birds. Flocks range from a pair of birds to upwards of 10,000 individuals.

habitat: The natural home or environment of a bird.

hatchlings: Baby birds that have recently emerged from their eggs.

hood: The markings on the head of a bird, resembling a hood.

horns: A tuft or collection of feathers, usually on top of a bird's head, resembling horns.

host: A bird species that takes care of the eggs and babies of other bird species. See *brood parasites*.

incubation: The process of sitting on bird eggs in the nest to keep them warm until they hatch.

iridescent: A luminous, or bright, quality of feathers, with colors seeming to change when viewed from different angles.

jute: A string of rough fibers made from plants.

juvenile: A bird that isn't an adult yet.

lard: Fat from a pig.

lore: The area on each side of a bird's face between the eye and the base of the bill.

migrate: The regular, predictable pattern of seasonal movement by some birds from one region to another, especially to escape winter.

molt: The process of dropping old, worn-out feathers and replacing them with new feathers, usually only one feather at a time.

morph: A bird with a color variation. Morphs also sometimes occur in mammals, reptiles, amphibians and insects.

mute: The inability to make or produce audible sounds. The Turkey Vulture (pg. 35), for example, is mostly mute.

nape: The back of a bird's neck.

necklace: The markings around the neck of a bird, as seen in the Western Meadowlark (pg. 219).

nectar: A sugar and water solution found in plants and flowers.

plumage: The collective set of feathers on a bird at any given time.

poster board: A stiff cardboard that is used in projects, especially for displaying information.

prey: Any critter that is hunted and killed by another for food.

raptor: A flesh-eating bird of prey that hunts and kills for food. Hawks, eagles, ospreys, falcons, owls, and vultures are raptors. See *prey*.

regurgitate: The process of bringing swallowed food up again to the mouth to feed young birds.

rendered: Animal fat that has been reduced or melted down by heating and then strained in order to make it pure.

sap: The watery liquid that moves up and down within the circulatory system of a tree, carrying nutrients throughout.

silhouettes: Dark shapes or outlines against a lighter background.

speculum: A patch of bright feathers on some birds, such as ducks, found on the wings.

squab: A young pigeon or dove, usually still in the nest. See *nestlings*.

suet: Animal fat, usually beef, that has been heated and made into cakes to feed birds. See *rendered*.

thermals: A column of upward-moving warm air caused by the sun warming the earth. Raptors and other birds gain altitude during flight by "riding" on thermals.

trachea: A large tubelike organ that allows air to pass between the lung and the mouth of a bird. Also called a windpipe.

trill: A fluttering or repeated series of similar-sounding musical notes given by some birds.

twitter: A high-pitched call of a bird. See *call*.

ultraviolet light: A kind of light that is visible to birds and insects but unseen by people.

vegetation: Any plants, especially those found growing in a particular habitat.

warble: A quiet bird song with many different sounds.

waterfowl: A group of similar birds with a strong connection to water. Ducks, geese, and others are examples of waterfowl.

CHECKLIST/INDEX BY SPECIES

Use the circles to checkmark the birds you've seen.